Cats

Cats

The best of the classic breeds

David Alderton

Featuring photographs

by Marc Henrie

BARNES
& NOBLE

NEW YORK

Editor: Ray Bonds
Design: Ian Hughes, Mousemat design

All photographs © Marc Henrie, except for page 19 © David Alderton, and those on pages 40-41, 42-45, 90-91, 106-107, 130-131, and 168-169 © Chanan Photography

2006 Barnes & Noble Publishing

ISBN-13: 978-0-7607-8500-3
ISBN-10: 0-7607-8500-7

Printed and bound in China

1 3 5 7 9 10 8 6 4 2

The Author

David Alderton is an international best-selling authority on cats and their care, with his titles having sold over a million copies worldwide. His work has won a commendation from the Cat Writers' Association of America, while two of his books on cats were cited by the well known zoologist Dr. Desmond Morris as being in his personal list of "The 100 Best Cat Books" published since 1727. David contributes to a wide range of general and specialist publications about cats on a regular basis. A frequent participant in radio programs, often live phone-ins, David has also appeared on television on numerous occasions. He is a consultant for the Pet Industry Joint Advisory Council based in Washington, D.C., and has visited cat shows and breeders in the United States, as well as in mainland Europe, Japan, and Australia. He keeps Abyssinian and British Shorthair cats at home.

Additional photographs
Page 1: Mother and kitten Russian.
Pages 2-3: Leopard Bengal kittens
Pages 4-5: A Silver Tortie Tabby Maine Coon.
Pages 6-7: A Havana and a Lavender Oriental.
Pages 188-189: The striking Savannah.

CONTENTS

INTRODUCTION

THE RISING POPULARITY OF CATS

There are now more cats sharing our daily lives than ever before. This is partly because cats are generally easy to look after, thanks to their relatively independent and adaptable natures. As a result, cats can be kept in city apartments and, unlike dogs, they do not need to be taken out for daily walks. On the other hand, they will thrive just as well in suburban or rural environments.

Being easier to manage than a dog, a cat is also a more natural choice as a pet for someone living on their own with a busy lifestyle. If you are likely to be back late, for example, then you can leave sufficient food for your cat so that there is no risk of your pet going hungry. The provision of a litter tray should ensure that your cat does not soil in the home, and there are also plenty of toys available now, to keep your pet occupied in your absence. Conversely, though, a cat will be equally at home living with a family.

Just as the number of cats being kept as pets continues to grow, so too does the number of different breeds that are available, reflecting the thriving show scene that exists today. Having been bred to conform as closely as possible to specified criteria in terms of their appearance, pure-bred cats vary quite widely not just in the way that they look, but also in terms of their temperament too.

The differing personalities of the various breeds are a very important aspect to consider if you are thinking of acquiring a pure-bred cat as a pet. Their care may also be more involved and time-consuming, particularly with regard to their grooming needs, when compared with their non-pedigree counterparts. By studying the profiles provided in this book therefore, you should be able to find your ideal feline companion.

ABOVE: The playful nature of cats is part of their appeal.

RIGHT: Cats today appear in a wide range of coat types and colors. This is a Chinchilla Persian.

INDOORS AND OUT

Cats like to roam outdoors exploring, but they can be just as happy in the home. Especially in city areas over recent years, many cat-owners have therefore decided to adapt their homes so that they can keep their cats indoors permanently. This is a reflection of the dangers that cats can face in urban areas today. Whereas advances in veterinary care have meant that cats can potentially live longer than ever before, many end up being badly injured or dying prematurely on roads close to where they live, particularly at night.

Cats as hunters have highly developed senses to help them to locate their quarry, becoming more active at dusk. Their hearing is very acute, enabling them to detect the high-pitched sounds uttered by rodents that are inaudible to our ears. Their vision too is superior to ours, especially at night, but this is sadly what can prove to be their undoing.

They have a reflective layer known as the *tapetum lucidum* at the back of the retina of each eye, where the image forms. Unfortunately, if a cat is crossing the road after dark, it can become easily dazzled by a vehicle's headlights, so that it does not see the approaching danger.

The situation is made worse by the fact that cats display no road sense. Even after being involved in a collision of this type, a cat will not be aware of the threat in the future. There are steps that you can take as an owner though, to try to safeguard your pet from traffic. Encourage your cat to come in at night, and have your pet neutered, which should reduce his or her desire to wander off. You can also obtain a special elasticated collar with a flashing light or a reflective band, which may give a driver more warning of your cat's presence.

LEFT: A cat will readily sleep on a chair or sofa in the home.

RIGHT: Cats often take the opportunity to sunbathe outdoors.

STARTING OUT

Many people starting out in search of a cat will want to acquire a kitten. If you are seeking a pure-bred companion, then the likelihood is that you will need to find a breeder, who may be tracked down through advertisements in the various cat magazines. On the other hand, rescue centers have a selection of ordinary non-pedigree kittens seeking homes. Pure-bred kittens can go to new homes by the time they are about three months old, although other kittens may be weaned slightly earlier.

You will need to decide whether you want a male or female kitten. If you are simply seeking a pet, this will make little difference because you will need to have your cat neutered by the time that he or she is five months old. If the cat is not neutered, you

are likely to be faced by behavioral problems such as soiling around the home, not to mention unwanted kittens if you have a female cat. For show and breeding purposes, however, a female will be a better option.

If you want cats to keep each other company, then it will be better to start with two kittens, because trying to introduce older individuals together is often fraught with difficulty. Kittens that have grown up together will retain a strong bond throughout their lives, playing together and grooming each other readily.

You may find yourself drawn to an older cat though. Rescue centers often have great difficulty in finding good homes for such cats, even in the case of those that have lived as pets throughout their lives, rather than being strays.

The only drawback of having an older individual is that the cat's age may be unknown, but it will certainly not take long for you to win your new pet's confidence. It will be important to keep the cat indoors for at least two weeks though, so that it comes to recognize its new home. Kittens cannot be allowed out for a similar period, until after they are fully vaccinated.

LEFT: Littermates get along well together.

RIGHT: Cats that are family members retain a close bond.

MAKING A CHOICE

Most cats in search of new homes at a rescue center will be non-pedigree, although they might well be first generation crosses, resulting from the matings between pure-breds and non-pedigree cats, so that they show clear features of their pure-bred ancestor. Since they will all be highly individual in terms of their appearance, so it can be very difficult to make a choice. Be guided by what the staff say about the individual cats, as they will be aware of their temperaments and backgrounds. They will want to ensure that your new cat settles well with you.

Bright eyes and a clean nose indicate good health.

Start out with some set parameters though. If you do not feel that protracted grooming is something that appeals to you, then clearly it will be better to seek out a shorthaired cat, rather than a longhair. This may give you more time to play with your pet instead.

Try to watch also how the cats react to you. Just like any relationship, living with a

cat is a two-way process, and it helps if your cat bonds well with you from the outset, although most cats are fairly adaptable when it comes to associating with people. You do need to bear in mind that, with luck, this is a relationship that will last for well over a decade, and so it is not a decision to be rushed, particularly if you are at all uncertain.

You will need to know as much as possible about your new pet, whether an adult cat or kitten, in terms of immunizations and deworming needs. It is especially important not to change your new pet's food suddenly, as this can lead to digestive disorders. Instead, you should make changes gradually, after several weeks.

The scene at a cat sanctuary or rehoming center.

SETTLING-IN

Cats of all ages will soon settle in new surroundings, particularly if you develop a routine. However, if you are introducing a newcomer to the home alongside an existing cat, this may be more problematic. There is simply no guarantee as to how two unfamiliar cats will act together. You are likely to find that your existing pet seeks to reinforce its territorial dominance around the home by soiling here, when confronted by a newcomer.

Never try to force the cats together, but allow them to get to know each other gradually, so as to minimize the risk of conflict. Over a period of time, the cats should come to accept each other, but as to whether they form a close bond, washing each other and feeding together in due course, will be hard to predict. There are most likely to be disagreements at first over mealtimes, so that it is a good idea to feed them separately. You can then keep a check on their individual appetites, and ensure that your established pet is not stealing food from the newcomer.

With a kitten on its own, you may want to have a crate in the home where you can keep your pet securely while it is young, and feed it here as well. It is important to provide a quiet

Harmony in a multi-cat household.

locality, so your cat can eat undisturbed. Fresh drinking water should always be available, but there is no need to give your cat milk.

Some cats, particularly those of Oriental origins such as Siamese, actually lack the enzyme known as lactase and so they cannot digest the milk sugar known as lactose. This ferments in their intestinal tract and gives them diarrhea.

Cats generally are very clean by nature, and by the time a kitten is ready to come to a new home it is likely to be using a litter tray, so simply make sure this is within easy reach. A kitten will usually use its litter tray after eating and when it wakes from a sleep.

ABOVE: Always wash the food bowl between meals.

BELOW: Check that cats each receive enough food.

VISITING THE VET

Soon after you acquire your new pet, you will need to make an appointment to visit the veterinarian. You must also obtain a secure carrier that you can use to move your cat. This will also be helpful when you go away on vacation, and your pet needs to be taken to a boarding cattery, or if you enter a show. Cats generally have a reputation for disliking traveling, but this is frequently because they do not become familiar with the experience from an early age and so become very distressed by it later in life. Show cats, which are used to being moved in this way from an early age, do not display this fear.

There are various types of cat carrier available. Those that allow your cat to travel in relative darkness are better, providing more seclusion. Always line the interior with old newspaper, and place a blanket on top, so your cat will be comfortable. Be sure too that the door is securely closed.

After your initial visit, you will need to return to your vet at least once a year, so that your cat's routine vaccinations against cat flu and other illnesses can be kept current. Take care of the vaccination certificate too, because you will need to have this when you take your pet to a cattery, for example.

Depending on where you live, and also if you intend to travel abroad, your cat may also need to be vaccinated against rabies. Microchipping is also a good idea, as a means of identifying your pet in case it strays. The microchip is located inside a tiny capsule about the size of a rice grain, and contains a unique code number that can be read by a scanner. It is inserted under the cat's skin by your vet, in a similar way to giving an injection.

Regular deworming is also very important, particularly if your cat is a hunter, and treatment for fleas will be needed as well, especially since cats sometimes acquire tapeworms from fleas.

RIGHT: Cats should be vaccinated as kittens, and annually thereafter.

BELOW: Modern veterinary care helps to prevent illnesses.

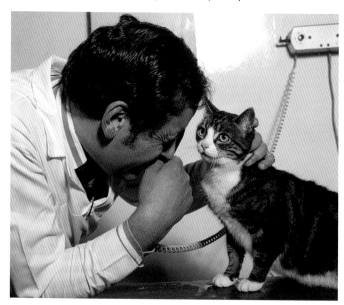

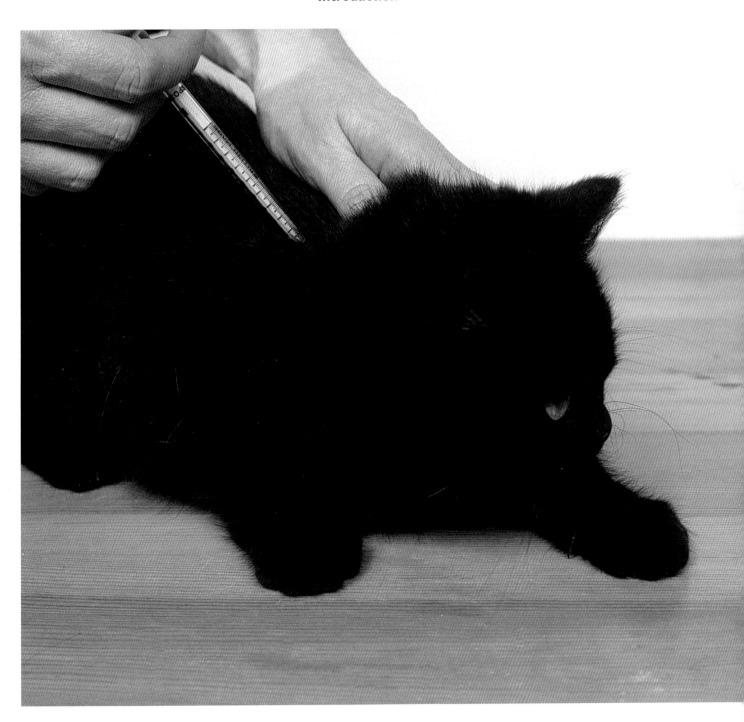

GROOMING

The major difference in caring for shorthaired and longhaired cats lies in the amount of grooming that they require. A cat's coat is typically made up of three different types of hair. The down lies closest to the body, and helps to provide insulation. Above this are the awn hairs, while the longest, most conspicuous hairs in the coat are the primary guard hairs.

Changes in the length and arrangement of any of these hairs affect the cat's appearance. Breeds that developed in warm countries, such as the Siamese, do not have any significant down hairs, and so their coat is very sleek, lying close to the body and outlining their muscular profile.

On the other hand, breeds such as the Maine Coon, originating naturally from cold climates, have a thick undercoat and a

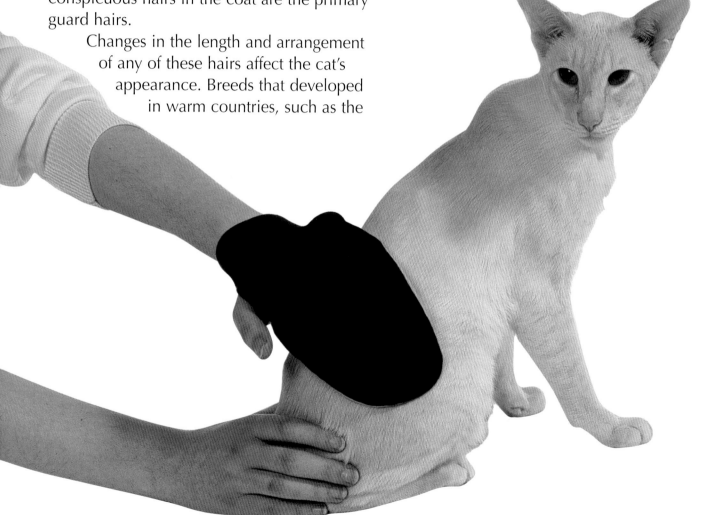

weather-resistant top coat. The coats of these cats show seasonal variations, being thicker during the winter months in temperate climates. Then, in the spring, much of the dense undercoat is shed. This can transform their appearance, as they will tend to lose the long ruff of fur. In some cases, as with the Turkish Angora, the coat will then resemble that of a shorthair through the summer months. This is why they are called semi-longhairs.

Longhaired cats need daily grooming, to prevent their coats from becoming tangled. This is especially important when shedding is occurring, to remove the loose hairs and prevent them being deposited on furniture and carpeting around the home. It will also help to protect your pet from hairballs, to which longhaired cats in particular can be susceptible.

As a general guide with longhaired cats, groom against the natural lie of the fur first, to strip out the lose hairs, before grooming the coat down again. If mats do form in the coat, take care not to pull on these, since this will be painful for your cat. If you cannot tease them apart, you may have to cut them out. Shorthaired cats can simply be combed in the direction of the lie of the fur.

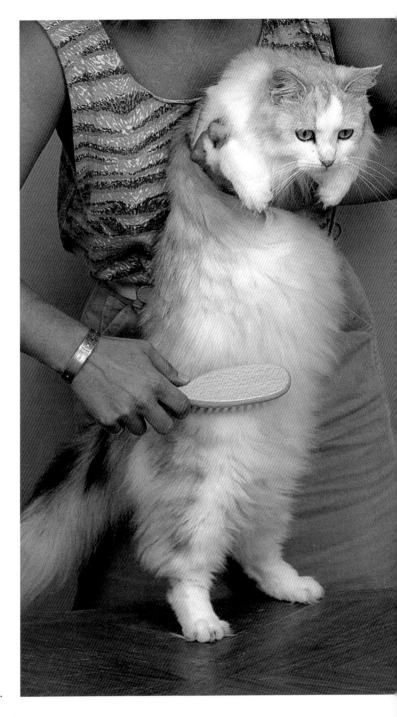

LEFT: Using a velvet glove will give a good gloss to the coat of a shorthaired cat.

RIGHT: Do not neglect the underparts when grooming your cat.

WATCH YOUR CAT'S BEHAVIOR !

Cats will instinctively spend long periods washing and grooming their coats, using their paws to wipe the sides of their faces and back of the neck, which they cannot lick themselves. This is not without its hazards though, because it means that cats can be very vulnerable to any harmful substances that contaminate the coat. These may be licked off and swallowed.

Longhaired cats are likely to swallow hairs as they groom themselves. This is because the rough surface of the cat's tongue acts rather like a rasp, pulling the hairs out of the coat and causing them to stick here, so that they end up being swallowed. In the stomach, the hairs start to coalesce into a mat, creating a partial blockage known as a hairball.

The most obvious sign of this will be evident from your cat's behavior, with your pet seemingly constantly hungry, going back and forth to its food bowl but only eating small amounts. Treatment generally consists of giving a laxative to clear this obstruction, but the best solution is to use a special food containing an ingredient that reduces the risk, as well as grooming your cat to remove loose hairs.

If your cat spends longer than normal apparently biting at his coat, this is often indicative of the presence of fleas. You will need a special fine-toothed flea comb to find evidence of these parasites. It will be better to groom the cat outdoors, so that if any fleas

do leap off they are less likely to infest your pet again. Dark specks in the fur are indicative of their presence, being the undigested remains of the cat's blood, on which fleas have fed. Aside from treating your cat with a suitable preparation to kill fleas, wash your pet's bedding and vacuum around the bed to remove immature fleas as well.

Cats have a reputation for sleeping for longer than any other mammal. Kittens and older cats in particular may sleep for up to eighteen hours every day. This is quite normal behavior, and not a cause for concern.

ABOVE: Persistent nibbling may indicate fleas.

LEFT: Even young kittens will groom themselves.

ABOVE: Cats can sleep in unlikely positions.

CATS AS ATHLETES

Cats are very playful by nature, and are supreme athletes, being able to climb and jump with ease. As a result, it is a good idea to put any particularly valuable ornaments in a glass cabinet or transfer them to a part of the home from where your cat is excluded, so as to prevent any risk of them being knocked off and broken.

As a way of deterring your cat from climbing on furniture, you could invest in a special indoor climbing frame, of which there are various designs available. These often incorporate other items too, such as a scratching post, to deter a cat from sharpening its claws on the furniture, which is especially likely in the case of cats housed permanently indoors. Some climbing frames even incorporate dens too, where your cat can sleep.

Bear in mind that various household plants can prove to be hazardous to cats, particularly cacti with their sharp spines that may easily become embedded in the paw or nose of an inquisitive young cat. Should this happen, then your pet will probably need to be sedated by a vet to remove these spines. Other household plants may be toxic if your cat decides to nibble at them, and so keep them all out of your pet's reach.

Although cats are strictly carnivorous in their feeding habits, they will eat some vegetation occasionally, and this is why, for cats living permanently indoors, it is a good idea to provide them with a tray of grass for this purpose. Kits of this type are available from pet stores: do not use ordinary lawn grass seed, because this is often treated with potentially toxic chemicals. Eating grass, especially coarse stems, can often be a sign of a hairball, however, so beware, because the grass may act as an emetic, encouraging the cat to regurgitate the mat of fur from its stomach.

ABOVE: Cats will extend their reach by standing up on their hind legs.

RIGHT: This Lavender Burmese could knock over an ornament.

OUT AND ABOUT

Cats will climb not only in the home, but will also frequently do so outdoors. Owners sometimes become worried that their cat may be trapped up a tree, but even if the cat has climbed up there to avoid a pursuing dog, for example, it will be able to come down by itself once it feels safe. Young cats in particular are most likely to appear as if they are marooned up a tree, simply because they may be less confident about coming down.

This is a reflection of the fact that it is much easier for a cat than other animals to climb up a tree. It uses its claws, rather like a mountaineer uses crampons, to haul itself up the bark, and then it can rest on a horizontal branch once it feels safe. When going down though, a cat needs to clamber backwards, which is not just harder but also means that it may feel more vulnerable. Once close to ground level, the cat will turn round, and jump the last few feet down back to earth.

Some cats tend to spend longer climbing than others, with lighter breeds such as Siamese being more inclined to roam through the trees, just like their wild ancestors. They can be sufficiently adept to hunt in these surroundings, catching birds and even other creatures such as lizards here, off the ground. As they grow older however, so cats become less inclined to climb regularly.

Cats do have a remarkable head for heights. Even if they lose their grip or misjudge a leap off the ground, then their incredible reflexes can save them from serious injury or even death. If a cat slips while off the ground, then the semi-circular canals in the ears, acting as organs of balance, ensure that its body swivels instantaneously so that it lands on its feet, minimizing the risk of injury. In the case of falls from high windows though, cats can suffer broken jaws, because of the momentum of the impact, but they usually still survive.

ABOVE: Cats such as this Oriental will climb readily.

LEFT: Cats seem quite comfortable in even the most precarious of places.

RIGHT: Cats can turn themselves right-side up as they fall to the ground.

ENSURING A LONG LIFE

Cats can make great companions for people of all ages, and studies are actually revealing the benefits to us of sharing our lives with a pet cat. Simply stroking a cat can help to lower your blood pressure, while caring for a cat helps young people to develop a sense of social awareness from an early age.

The bond between owner and cat today is also likely to last longer than ever before. The life expectancy of cats has grown dramatically over recent years thanks to a better understanding of their nutritional needs, combined with improved health care. Many kittens born today will probably live well into their late teens and possibly into their early twenties.

Aim to ensure that your pet has a healthy lifestyle though, by being neutered and keeping its vaccinations up to date. In the case of male cats especially, this surgery has the additional advantage of minimizing the risk that your pet might become injured as the result of fighting. During such encounters, cats can acquire potentially deadly infections such as Feline AIDS, which attacks the feline immune system, although it is not an infection related to the human illness.

It is also vital to ensure that your cat does not become overweight, which is especially likely from middle age onwards. This could otherwise have serious effects on its health, just as in people, being linked with conditions such as heart disease and diabetes. Switching an older cat to a diet specially formulated for seniors at about seven years old is therefore to be recommended. Foods of this type will not just have a lower calorie content, reflecting your pet's less active lifestyle, but they will also have other key ingredients that should help to offset the effects of the aging process for as long as possible, aiding a cat's mobility as well.

ABOVE: Owners of all ages can enjoy the company of a cat.

RIGHT: A young girl with her Silver Tabby kitten.

SHORTHAIRED CATS

British Blue Shorthair—a popular variety today.

Although the way in which cats are classified for show purposes may differ somewhat between individual organizations, quite apart from countries, the breeds themselves are broadly split into shorthaired and longhaired divisions.

Actual recognition of breeds is a relatively recent phenomenon, dating back just over a hundred years, to a time when organized cat shows were beginning. Since those early days, the number of breeds has grown dramatically, to the extent that there are over eighty in existence now, although some are very rare.

Breeds come about in various ways. There are those that have a long history, originating over a millennium in some cases, as with a number of the Asiatic breeds such as the Korat and Siamese. They now possess highly distinctive, recognizable characteristics, having been bred in isolation over this period. In the case of these traditional breeds, which include others from the far north, such as the Norwegian Forest Cat, their appearance has clearly been shaped to an extent by the environment in which they have developed.

Other breeds have evolved as the result of spontaneous mutations cropping up in litters alongside ordinary cats. This group includes some of the most striking of all of today's cat breeds, such as the virtually hairless Sphynx and the various rex breeds, not to mention the short-legged Munchkin. Establishing such breeds is a fraught process though, with no guarantee of success, as the mutation might be lost in the early stages.

Then there have been refinements based on breeding ordinary street cats, which have given rise to both the American and British Shorthair breeds. Crossings of different breeds have also swelled the numbers of those available today, with matings between American Shorthairs and Persian Longhairs leading on to the Exotic breed, as an example.

In other cases though, crossings of this type have been used much more judiciously, to introduce a particular color to a breed, rather than alter the physical appearance or so-called "type" of the breed itself.

Most recently, there has been a new trend in cat breeding, which has resulted in cross-breeding between domestic and small wild cats. Already, the Bengal breed has become well established as a result, and others such as the Savannah are now starting to become more common.

Non-pedigree Shorthair

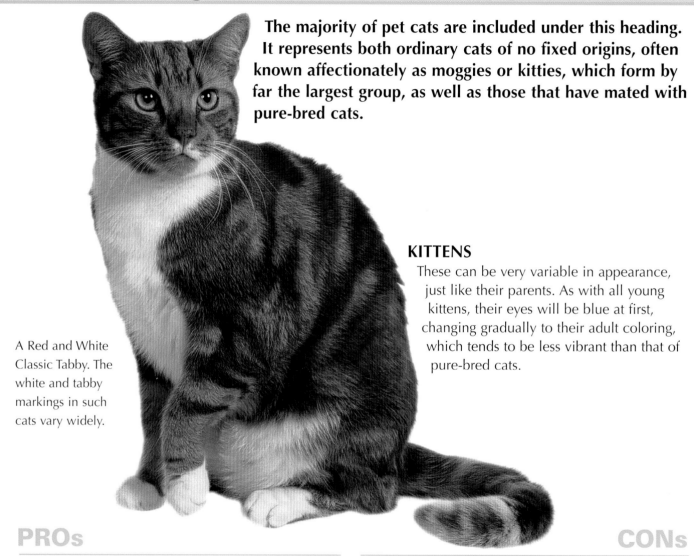

The majority of pet cats are included under this heading. It represents both ordinary cats of no fixed origins, often known affectionately as moggies or kitties, which form by far the largest group, as well as those that have mated with pure-bred cats.

A Red and White Classic Tabby. The white and tabby markings in such cats vary widely.

KITTENS

These can be very variable in appearance, just like their parents. As with all young kittens, their eyes will be blue at first, changing gradually to their adult coloring, which tends to be less vibrant than that of pure-bred cats.

PROs

- Complete individual appearance
- Usually healthy and hardy
- Adaptable nature
- Inexpensive to obtain

CONs

- Very likely to display tabby and/or white markings
- Hard to predict adult size
- May be inclined to wander
- Often effective hunters

BREED PROFILE

Basic type: Shorthaired and relatively smooth-coated, depending on ancestry. Compact, well-built with a muscular body.

Size: Generally medium, but can be variable.

Colors: Tend to correspond to those seen naturally in European breeds, such as brown, black, blue, red ("ginger"). Bicolors and tabby variants, especially mackerel and tabby forms of these colors, are prevalent.

Coat: Usually quite short and dense, with a firm, resilient texture.

Body: Medium-sized, powerful, with a straight back and relatively short legs.

Tail: Medium length, tapering tail, often quite broad at the base.

Head: A rounded face shape is fairly typical, with males developing evident jowls as they mature, creating the impression of a double chin. The nose is short and straight, and there is often a white facial blaze between the eyes. The ears are usually quite small and widely spaced.

Eyes: Relatively large and rounded, differing significantly in coloration between individuals.

Life expectancy: 14-17 years.

SHOW STANDARD

There is no established show standard for such cats, because of their variation in appearance, as they do not have a recognizable type. Nevertheless, they can be exhibited in classes alongside each other at some shows, where they will be judged on features such as their condition and friendliness.

Brown Non-pedigree. This coloration is closest to that of the domestic cat's original wild ancestor.

Non-pedigree Shorthair

Origins

The original ancestor of all domestic cats is the African Wild Cat (*Felis lybica*), which is dark in color and has tabby patterning. These features are still apparent in many non-pedigree cats, which have changed very little in appearance over the course of millennia. The domestication process probably began in ancient Egypt, around 9,000 years ago. Such cats were taken around the Mediterranean, and then further north in Europe and east to Asia.

Tabby Markings

Just two types of tabby patterning are commonly seen in non-pedigree cats. The Classic is the ancestral form, with the darker tabby markings creating a very distinctive blotch on the flanks. This contrasts with the Mackerel Tabby, where narrow stripes run evenly down the sides of the body. In either case, there is likely to be an M-shaped tabby marking on the forehead, barring on the legs, and stripes present on the tail.

A Red Mackerel Tabby. The fine-lined pattern is a feature of this tabby variety.

Random Patterning

There was no attempt to breed cats selectively for their coloration or appearance right up until the end of the 1800s, when cat showing started to become a fashionable pastime. As breeders then sought to create cats with particular characteristics, so they used these non-pedigree individuals, selecting for features that appealed to them. Both the British and American Shorthaired breeds were created in this way.

Today's Bicolor British Shorthairs, for example, now show remarkable consistency in the colored and white areas of their coat, compared with non-pedigree cats that displayed random patterning of this type. Breeders also sought to remove the tabby markings, which are a feature of virtually all ordinary, non-pedigree cats, to create

what are now known as "selfs." These cats have pure coloring, displaying no tabby markings.

However, red pure-bred kittens often still display faint signs of tabby patterning on their coats at first, reflecting their ancestry, although these usually fade with age. Breeders also tended to select for cats of deeper coloration in this case too, so that non-pedigree red cats are often called gingers, whereas the coloration of their pure-bred counterparts is described as red.

Brown Mackerel and White. All non-pedigrees have random markings, making them highly individual pets.

Abyssinian

Affectionate, intelligent and alert, the Abyssinian will prove to be an excellent family companion, cohabiting well with dogs as well as being tolerant with children. It is also a very playful breed, and this activity will help to reinforce the bond between you.

Ruddy or Usual Abyssinian. This is an athletic breed.

KITTENS

It is often hard to assess the show potential of a young Abyssinian kitten, because the coats of these cats are relatively dark at birth, and it will take several months before its adult coloration becomes evident.

PROs

- Beautiful appearance
- Very affectionate and loyal
- Good range of colors
- Coat requires very little grooming

CONs

- Relatively small litters
- Patience may be required to obtain a particular color
- Relatively susceptible to feline leukemia
- Not all new colors accepted at shows

Chocolate—one of the newer Abyssinian colors.

BREED PROFILE

Basic type: Shorthaired, with a relatively long, lithe body.

Size: Medium.

Colors: Include ruddy (also known as the "usual"), sorrel, blue, chocolate, lavender, cream, red, fawn, black silver, blue silver and sorrel silver, usual tortie, sorrel tortie, blue tortie, chocolate tortie, lilac tortie and fawn tortie.

Coat: Fine, with a soft and silky texture, and shiny in appearance. Also has a dense texture, which makes it quite resilient.

Body: Graceful yet muscular without being coarse. Intermediate in size between the cobby nature of the British Shorthair and the svelte profile of the Orientals.

Tail: Relatively long, tapering along its length from a thick base.

Head: Slightly rounded, wedge-shaped. There is a slight stop between the forehead and the bridge of the nose. Muzzle is quite compact.

Eyes: Large and almond-shaped, highlighted by dark skin of the lids, with a surrounding paler area.

Life expectancy: 13-16 years.

SHOW STANDARD

Must not display any sign of a white locket on the chest, although white on the chin and upper throat area is acceptable. The body shape must not be cobby, and the tail must always have a dark tip.

Abyssinian

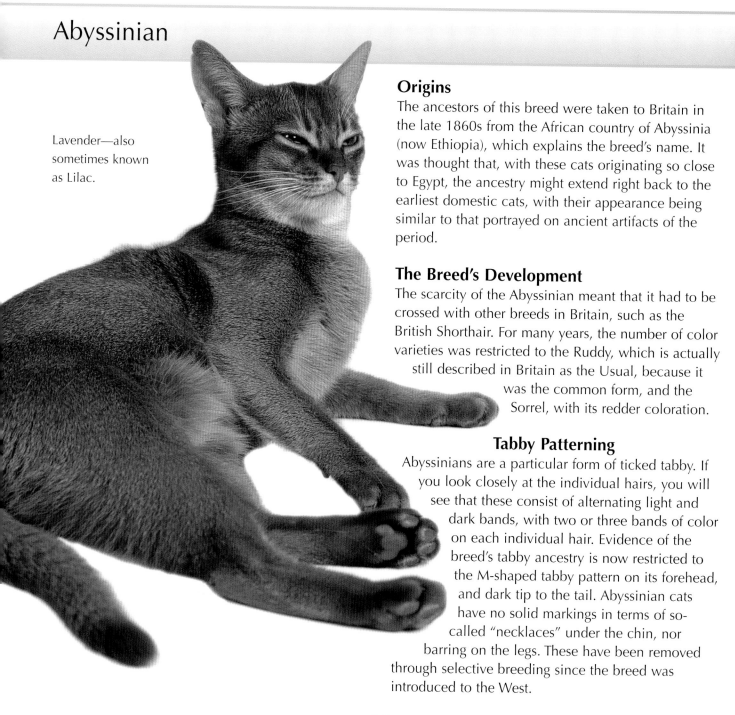

Lavender—also sometimes known as Lilac.

Origins

The ancestors of this breed were taken to Britain in the late 1860s from the African country of Abyssinia (now Ethiopia), which explains the breed's name. It was thought that, with these cats originating so close to Egypt, the ancestry might extend right back to the earliest domestic cats, with their appearance being similar to that portrayed on ancient artifacts of the period.

The Breed's Development

The scarcity of the Abyssinian meant that it had to be crossed with other breeds in Britain, such as the British Shorthair. For many years, the number of color varieties was restricted to the Ruddy, which is actually still described in Britain as the Usual, because it was the common form, and the Sorrel, with its redder coloration.

Tabby Patterning

Abyssinians are a particular form of ticked tabby. If you look closely at the individual hairs, you will see that these consist of alternating light and dark bands, with two or three bands of color on each individual hair. Evidence of the breed's tabby ancestry is now restricted to the M-shaped tabby pattern on its forehead, and dark tip to the tail. Abyssinian cats have no solid markings in terms of so-called "necklaces" under the chin, nor barring on the legs. These have been removed through selective breeding since the breed was introduced to the West.

Longhaired Kittens

Occasionally, a longhaired kitten may crop up in a litter of Abyssinians. This is an indication that both Abyssinian parents are carrying the longhaired gene, although it will not be apparent from their appearance. Such longhaired kittens are now recognized as a separate breed, called the Somali (see pages 178-81).

Silvers

In the case of Silver varieties of the Abyssinian, the undercoat is always white, and this creates a distinct contrast with the top coat. It has not proved particularly easy to breed good examples, because any lingering hint of darker barring will be highlighted by the white undercoat. Not all cat organizations currently accept Silver Abyssinians as a result.

The Sorrel Silver's coloration is silvery-peach, with chocolate ticking.

American Curl

These highly distinctive cats are all descended from a single stray kitten that was rescued in Lakewood, California, in 1981. They are therefore essentially not highly developed, in terms of their type, but have retained a natural appearance, and have a very friendly, approachable character.

Shorthaired American Curls are a very distinctive breed. This is a tabby variant.

KITTENS

It is impossible to distinguish at first those kittens that will have the distinctive curled ears, simply because all are born with normal ears. Signs should be apparent by the time that the kittens are about a week old. The curling itself is a gradual process, which takes place over several months.

PROs

- A very distinctive breed
- No specific care concerns
- Very affectionate cats by nature
- Playful temperament
- Bred in many colors

CONs

- Energetic, needs space to exercise
- Not widely available
- A particular color may be hard to find
- Likely to wander outdoors
- Longhaired examples can occur in litters as well

BREED PROFILE

Basic type: Shorthaired, with a semi-foreign type. Elegant, with a well proportioned body.

Size: Medium.

Colors: Any colors or patterns are acceptable in this breed, including colorpoints.

Coat: Short, with virtually no undercoat. Has a fine, silky texture. Ear furnishings—hair within the ears themselves—stick out from the folds and are clearly apparent. Desirable lynx-like tufts of hair may also be evident on the tips of the ears.

Body: Intermediate between the classic foreign appearance of the Siamese and the cobby shape of the American Shorthair. The legs are relatively thick.

Tail: Relatively long, but proportionate to the body.

Head: Wedge-shaped, but with a reasonable length of muzzle, being longer than it is wide. The ears themselves are relatively large and rounded at the tips, which should point to the midline of the body.

Eyes: Large, colorful, and walnut-shaped. Colorpoints must have blue eyes.

Life expectancy: 12-15 years.

SHOW STANDARD

The distinctive curling results from a dominant gene, so matings between Curls and cats with normal ears are likely to result in approximately half the kittens having curled ears. Those that have normal ears are described by breeders as American Curl Straight Ears.

The patterning of these cats can vary noticeably, as shown by these two Ticked Tabby and White littermates.

American Shorthair

These hardy cats are very popular in their homeland, but are not generally seen elsewhere in the world. They make excellent companions, however, and are also very successful at shows, where their steady temperament means that they adapt quickly to the temporary change in their environment.

KITTENS

Closely resemble adults although their eyes are blue at first. These will start to change to their desired color when the kittens are about eight weeks old.

A Calico American Shorthair. Such cats are almost invariably female.

PROs

- Easy to care for
- A wide choice of colors
- Playful nature
- Stunning patterning
- Often long-lived

CONs

- Likes to roam outdoors
- Blue-eyed whites will be deaf
- Can be a keen hunter
- Sheds more heavily in spring
- Some varieties may be harder to find

BREED PROFILE

Basic type: Shorthaired, smooth-coated. Relatively large, with a rectangular body shape. The overall impression should be well balanced.

Size: Medium to large.

Colors: All the typical solid colors, such as white, cream, red, blue, black, plus classic (blotched) tabby, mackerel tabby, spotted tabby, tortie, torbie (tortie tabby), calico (tortoiseshell and white), tipped and shaded, smoke, and van-patterned variants.

Coat: Short and dense, with a harsh texture. Shiny and close-lying.

Body: Medium to large in size, with a broad chest, a long body shape, and rounded rump. The neck is in proportion to the body. Females are smaller than males. The legs are of medium length, with rounded paws.

Tail: Medium length, tapers slightly down to a rounded tip.

Head: Broad and rounded in shape, with males having definite jowls, with a relatively short, square muzzle. The ears are widely spaced, medium in terms of size, and rounded at their tips.

Eyes: Rounded, relatively widely spaced, with the color of the eyes corresponding to that of the coat.

Life expectancy: 12-15 years.

SHOW STANDARD

Patterning in the case of types such as tabbies needs to be well defined. The coat often becomes somewhat thicker during the winter months. Oriental colors such as chocolate and lilac, as well as colorpoint markings, are not permitted in this breed.

A Brown Classic Tabby and White.

American Shorthair

Origins

In the very early days of their existence, these cats developed as the result of random matings between the different shorthaired cats brought from Europe. Being what were simply ordinary kitties at this stage, they were ignored at the first United States cat shows, where breeds such as Persians and Abyssinians were to be seen. When the American Shorthair was finally accepted, however, it was described simply under the name of Shorthair, and this was subsequently changed to Domestic Shorthair.

Further Development

Many exhibitors tended to ignore these cats down the intervening decades, preferring more exotic breeds. But then, in the early 1960s, people in the cat world were forced to reassess their attitude towards this original American breed. In 1965, a stunning Silver Tabby won the coveted Cat of the Year Award, and soon the breed's name was changed again, to American Shorthair, to reflect its heritage. This placed it on a par with the British and European Shorthair breeds.

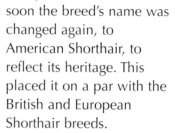

Silver Classic Tabby— also known as a Blotched Tabby, because of its markings.

Much more emphasis was then placed on developing the breed on similar lines to its European counterparts, with a similar breeding program being undertaken. Persians were used to increase the overall size of the American Shorthair, and they also added to the range of available color varieties. These matings also resulted in the unexpected creation of the Exotic (see pages 78-81) during this period. The rounded shape of the American Shorthair's head was also improved at this stage by carefully controlled Burmese matings, which also contributed to the breed's stocky appearance.

Since then, with its type firmly established, no outcrossings with other breeds are usually permitted. The end result today is that the American Shorthair has become a clearly defined breed. It can be distinguished from the British Shorthair by its longer body and nose, and a face that is less round.

Red Classic Tabby.

Bengal

Now ranking as one of the most popular breeds in the world, the Bengal is actually a relatively newcomer on the cat scene, and has an unusual ancestry. It was the first breed created through hybridization, as the result of cross-breeding between domestic cats and the Asian leopard cat (*Felis bengalensis*).

A Brown Spotted Bengal. These are powerful cats.

KITTENS

Bengal kittens' coats are usually slightly longer on average than those of adults, with the spotting being less apparent as a result, until they are about four months old. The coat will not feel as soft either, at this early age.

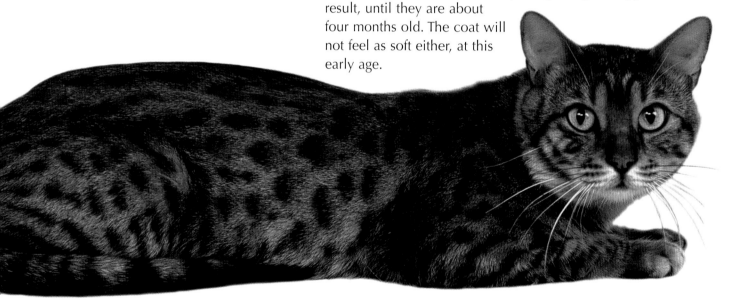

PROs

- Beautiful coat patterning
- Available in an increasing range of colors
- Gets along well with other cats and dogs
- Lively and inquisitive by nature
- Very playful

CONs

- Active and needs plenty of space
- Larger than most other breeds
- Not especially cuddly as companions
- Expensive
- Can be vulnerable to kidney disease

BREED PROFILE

Basic type: Shorthaired, with a very dense coat. Solidly built and muscular, being a powerful cat.

Size: Large.

Colors: An increasing range is being developed. More traditional varieties now include sorrel, which typically has an orange ground color with darker brown spotting, and mink, with black on a mahogany background. Crosses involving Siamese have created striking snow varieties, with lighter-colored coats. Both spotted and striped patterning are now recognized.

Coat: Smooth, with a soft, silky texture.

Body: Long and creates an impression of strength, with the legs being well boned and having large, round paws. The front legs are shorter than the hindlegs.

Tail: Medium in length, sturdy and with a rounded tip, which must always be dark in color.

Head: Relatively small, compared with the body, and wedge-shaped, with its length exceeding its width. The whisker pads on each side of the nose should be very evident. The nose is broad and long, with a slight stop evident between the eyes.

Eyes: Vary slightly from almond-shaped to round, and are large in size.

Life expectancy: 12-16 years.

A Black and Gold Marbled, with characteristic striped patterning.

SHOW STANDARD

It can take up to a year for the full depth of the Bengal's coloration to emerge. Regular handling from kittenhood onwards is very important to ensure that these cats will not be fearful when being judged.

Bengal

Development of the Breed

The development of the Bengal breed began back in the 1950s as the result of a genetic experiment to investigate feline leukemia. The first serious attempt to transfer the attractive and very distinctive spotted patterning of the Asian Leopard Cat and create a new domestic breed then followed in 1963. A geneticist called Jean Sugden used a female Leopard Cat that she mated with an ordinary domestic cat, acquired from a rescue shelter. They produced one kitten, which was called Kin-kin and fostered to a litter of domestic cats. When mated back to her father in due course, there were both spotted and plain-colored kittens in her litter. This confirmed that the coat patterning had been successively transferred.

Entering the Show Scene

It was not until the 1970s that the breeding program really expanded, using a group of eight hybrid cats from the University of California. The breed, whose name now commemorates the scientific name of its wild cat ancestor, was exhibited for the first time in the United States during the 1980s, and started to be seen in Europe by the end of the decade.

Initial Infertility

Mating of two similar species together can give rise to hybrid offspring, but often, as was shown in this case, litter sizes are initially often much smaller than normal. In addition, the early Bengal males proved to be infertile, which meant that to develop the strain it was necessary to use domestic tom cats, to mate with the hybrid females. These problems have now been overcome, and Bengals are bred together.

Temperament

After the initial cross was made, all subsequent pairings have involved only hybrids or domestic cats. Apart from non-pedigrees, Abyssinians and Burmese contributed to the Bengal's early development. Breeders have concentrated on developing the personality of Bengals. In the early days, the hybrids displayed obvious wild cat behavior patterns, particularly in terms of being shy and less friendly than ordinary cats. Since then though, great emphasis has been placed on ensuring that the Bengal has developed into an outgoing, friendly cat.

Aquatic Interests

Bengals are cats that often display a fascination with water. It is thought that this interest is inherited from their wild ancestor, which is always found close to water, and may even hunt in streams and pools.

A group of Leopard
Bengal kittens, with
their black patterning
clearly visible.

Bombay

Placid, with a friendly, good-natured temperament, the Bombay actually deserves to be more popular. It will settle well in a family home, while also making an ideal companion for someone living on their own. The breed was conceived to resemble a miniature black panther in appearance.

The Bombay closely resembles the Burmese in terms of type.

KITTENS

Bombay kittens have blue eyes at first, which will turn gray before developing their adult coloration. Their coats may show faint tabby markings initially, and they tend to have a rusty-brown tinge on their fur too.

PROs

- Easy-care coat
- Stunning appearance
- Placid companion
- Gets along well with dogs
- Tolerant with children

CONs

- May not be easy to acquire
- Exists only in one color
- Not pure-breeding
- Variable eye color
- Assertive and will demand attention

BREED PROFILE

Basic type: Shorthaired, with a particularly sleek coat. Legs, body and tail are all in proportion to each other.

Size: Medium.

Color: Black only, which must be consistent in coloration to its roots.

Coat: Unique appearance, with a distinctive texture resembling satin. Must be fine and short, possessing the characteristic gleam of patent leather, lying very close to the body. Has almost no undercoat.

Body: Medium-bodied and muscular, with toms being larger than queens.

Tail: Medium-length and straight along its length, with no signs of any kink.

Head: Rounded overall, whether seen from the side or the front, and quite broad, with the eyes being widely spaced. Narrows slightly to form the short yet well-developed muzzle. When seen in profile, there is also a clear stop for the nose.

Eyes: Rounded in shape and a very distinctive color, can vary from gold but ideally should approximate as closely as possible to a deep coppery shade. They are quite large, and widely spaced.

Lifespan expectancy: 14-16 years.

Bombay. A composite breed, bred from Burmese and American Shorthairs.

SHOW STANDARD

Common faults relate to the Bombay's coloration, which may not always be black to the roots, sometimes retaining a brownish-black hue. Odd white hairs in the coat are also a major flaw. Cats with the deepest-colored eyes are likely to be preferred.

British Shorthair

This was one of the first recognized breeds to be developed, featuring prominently at the early cat shows of the late 1800s, and is still very popular today. As the development of the British Shorthair has continued, so it has become available in a very wide range of colors and patterns, with literally hundreds of different combinations being possible.

KITTENS
Most varieties resemble adults, but often in the case of self-colored kittens there may be traces of ghost markings, in terms of faint tabby patterning on their coats. This usually disappears as the cat grows older, but in some cases, especially with cream and red cats, such markings may not disappear entirely.

White British Shorthair with distinctive right blue eye and amber left eye.

PROs
- Cute, cuddly appearance
- Needs little grooming
- Relaxed temperament
- Hardy nature
- Bred in many colors and patterns

CONs
- Relatively large size
- Not all colors readily available
- Deafness afflicts some varieties
- Friendly even to strangers
- Rather prone to obesity

BREED PROFILE

Basic type: Shorthaired, with a dense coat. A relatively large breed, especially in the case of males, with a compact appearance.

Size: Medium to large.

Colors: Self colors include white, cream, chocolate, lilac, red, blue and black. There are also tortoiseshell variants, such as blue-cream, and tortie and white forms. There are many different varieties of tabby, which may display classic, mackerel, ticked or spotted patterning, and further combinations such as tortie tabbies too. Silver variants also exist, as do colorpoints, which are the latest development in this group.

Coat: Distinguishable by its short yet crisp texture.

Body: Cobby, with relatively short but strong, stocky legs. The chest is deep and broad, with the back being short and level.

Tail: Medium-length and thick, especially at the base, being rounded at the tip.

Head: Rounded, with mature toms having pronounced jowls that give the appearance of a double chin. The chin is strong and firm, with the nose being short. The ears are quite small, and have rounded tips.

Eyes: Well spaced, large and round.

Life expectancy: 13-16 years.

SHOW STANDARD

There must not be a pronounced nose stop in this breed. The texture of the coat is very important—it must not be either too long or fluffy either, and this applies to the tail too. Whisker pads should not be especially prominent, nor should the chin appear weak.

Black. Consistent, even coloration is a feature of "self" varieties.

British Shorthair

Origins

The British Shorthair is descended originally from the street cats of Victorian Britain. In order to emphasize the difference between them, breeders decided to increase the British Shorthair's size, and this was achieved by crossings with Persian Longhairs. Careful breeding then ensured that cats carrying longhaired genes did not play a significant part in the British Shorthair's subsequent development.

Creating New Varieties

Since those days, occasional crossings with Persians have been carried out at intervals. In more recent years, this has not been with a view to increasing the size of British Shorthairs, but as a way of creating new colors in the breed. Both Chocolate and Lilac were developed in this way, and then in turn these self colors have been used to breed other variants such as Chocolate and White Bicolors.

Blue and White Bicolor. There must be no intermingling of white and colored hairs.

Bicolors

One thing that sets British Shorthairs clearly apart from ordinary non-pedigree cats is the consistency of their markings, in the case of Bicolors as an example. In fact, the earliest standard drawn up for Bicolors, based on the Dutch breed of rabbit, was too demanding, so that breeders abandoned these varieties! Rather than calling for a banded appearance, therefore, such cats simply need somewhere between one third and a half of their fur to be white. Ideally, their markings should be symmetrical, and most importantly, the division between the colored and white areas of the coat should be clearly defined, with no odd white hairs present in the colored fur. Dark colors, such as black or blue, tend to be most commonly seen in Bicolors, because the contrast is greater with the areas of white in the coat.

Colorpoints

Colorpoints represent a new grouping within the British Shorthairs, which have become more prominent since the 1990s. Their distinctive patterning is the result of cross-breeding between British Shorthairs and Himalayans. Today, these cats have a typical pointed appearance, with darker coloring on the extremities of their bodies, such as the mask, ears, legs, feet, and tail offset against a significant paler body coloration, although, as with all pointed breeds, kittens are white at birth. There are not just self-pointed varieties such as the seal point, but tortie and tabby versions, as well as tortie tabbies, which are often called torbies. The tabby forms are also sometimes known as lynx points.

Tortoiseshell. This is essentially a female-only variety.

55

British Shorthair

White British Shorthairs

Within the Self division there are three separate white varieties, distinguishable on the basis of their eye coloration. There are the Blue-eyed and Orange-eyed forms, with acceptable coloration in the case of the Orange-eyed actually varying from deep gold through orange to copper. In the case of the Odd-eyed White, one eye is blue, again being of a deep sapphire shade, while the other is a variable shade of orange. Unfortunately, however, there is a genetic weakness linked with the blue-eyed coloration, which means that such cats are deaf. In the case of the Odd-eyed White, however, these cats do have normal hearing in the ear corresponding to the orange eye. It will be a matter of waiting until the kittens start to develop their mature adult eye coloration before being able to distinguish reliably between them, however, since all kittens have blue eyes at first.

Tortoiseshell Coloring

Thanks to another genetic quirk, almost all tortoiseshell cats are female, as in the case of the different forms of tortoiseshell that now exist in the British Shorthair. Although there is a tendency for pure-bred cats to be standardized in appearance, tortoiseshell varieties, as with tabbies and bicolors too, do have highly individual patterning. The standard Tortoiseshell is a combination of black, dark and light red, and this can also be broken with variable white coloration in some cases.

Lilac-cream Point Colorpoint—one of a growing number of Colorpoint varieties.

Silver Tabby. The contrast in the coat is very attractive.

Brown Mackerel Tabby, characterized by its thin striped patterning.

Burmese

Burmese cats are named after their homeland of Burma (Myanmar) in South-east Asia. They were traditionally a distinctive brown color, often described as sable, but over recent years other colors have been created too. The Burmese is an ideal choice as a companion for someone living on their own, as these cats thrive on attention.

Sable Burmese, which is the traditional color form.

KITTENS

Young Burmese may show traces of light tabby barring on their coats, up until the age of six months old. Their coat color is also paler than that of adults. Their eyes are blue initially, changing to gray-green, before developing their distinctive golden-yellow appearance.

PROs

- Affectionate by nature
- Playful disposition
- Grooming is very straightforward
- Very inquisitive
- Highly sociable

CONs

- Can be very vocal
- May become rather fretful if ignored
- Not all varieties are recognized universally for shows
- Eye color fades with age
- Matures early—beware of unwanted pregnancies

BREED PROFILE

Basic type: Shorthaired and with a sleek coat. Medium-sized, with an athletic build. Some regional variations, with North American Burmese being stockier than those seen in Europe.

Size: Medium, with toms being larger than queens.

Colors: Sable (brown), champagne (chocolate), platinum (lilac), blue. Other varieties include cream, red, plus lilac, chocolate, blue and black forms of tortoiseshell, which are seen more frequently in Europe than in North America.

Coat: Very short and sleek. Has a glossy appearance, with very little undercoat.

Body: Medium-length yet heavier than it may appear, with a rounded chest. Legs in proportion to the body. Oval paws.

Tail: Medium-length. Straight and quite slender. Does not taper significantly along its length, ending in a rounded tip.

Head: Rounded, with considerable width between the eyes. The ears are well spaced, carrying on the line of the face, and tilt forwards slightly. There is a distinctive nose break or stop, with the muzzle being short.

Eyes: Large and well spaced, with a rounded lower lid and a straight upper lid, slanting to the nose.

Life expectancy: 13-16 years.

SHOW STANDARD

It is very important that there is no deviation in the tail, resulting in any kinking along its length. Eye coloration is considered to be a very important feature and adult Burmese must never have greenish eyes, although the eye coloration of Blue Burmese especially fades with age.

Cream Burmese, with a rich cream coat color.

Burmese

Origins

The cat that is credited with being the founder of this breed in the West, called Wong Mau, was brought to the United States in 1930 by a Dr. Thompson, who had previously worked for the U.S. Navy. Three more examples of Burmese were obtained from Asia in 1942, and then in 1949 the breed was sent to England. There, greater emphasis was placed on increasing the available range of colors, partly because outcrossings to other breeds such as the Siamese had to be made, since the number of Burmese cats was very limited at that stage. Today, outcrosses are no longer permitted.

Meanwhile, breeders in the United States concentrated on the appearance of their existing Burmese. This helps to explain why, today, the number of color varieties recognized in the case of this breed is greater in Europe, and also why there is a divergence in their type, compared with those seen in North America. Indeed, some shows have separate classes for European-type Burmese, while the less traditional color forms of the Burmese are now often shown as Malayans.

Uneven Coloring

One of the features of the Burmese is that the coloration of the coat is not entirely even, becoming paler on the lower parts of the body. It is also quite usual for the mask and ears to appear slightly darker in color as well. As these cats grow older, so their overall coloration also tends to deepen.

Tortie Variants

These are basically a female-only group, for genetic reasons, and so these cats may appear slightly smaller in overall size. Their coloration is, however, considered to be less significant than their type. In Britain, where they originated, the aim is to avoid both an extreme Oriental appearance, as reflected by the Siamese, as well as the cobby form of the British Shorthair in the development of these and other Burmese variants.

LEFT: Red Burmese, displaying the desirable light tangerine shade.

LEFT: Chocolate Burmese—not to be confused with the Brown (Sable) variety.

ABOVE: These cats are (left to right) Cream, Blue, and Red Burmese.

Burmilla

These strikingly attractive cats came about as the result of a chance mating between a Lilac Burmese queen and a Silver Chinchilla Persian tom in 1981. Pigmentation extends further down the individual hairs in the case of Shaded Burmillas, compared with the corresponding Tipped variety.

Burmillas are characterized by a muscular appearance.

KITTENS

Burmilla kittens are often darker in coloration than adult cats, but the situation is confused since those with Burmese patterning as well are significantly lighter overall than their litter mates.

Distinguishing between Tipped and Shaded individuals can be difficult at this stage.

PROs

- Striking coloration
- Sound temperament
- Ideal family pet
- Very affectionate
- Grooming straightforward

CONs

- Relatively vocal
- Hard to predict ultimate appearance of adult cat
- Coat coloration may change again in older cats
- Eye coloration likely to fade
- One of the less common breeds

BREED PROFILE

Basic type: Shorthaired, smooth-coated. Muscular, and bearing a clear resemblance in type to that of its Burmese ancestor. Queens are smaller than toms.

Size: Medium.

Colors: Include either standard or silver coated varieties with cream, red, lilac, chocolate, blue, black, blue tortie, black tortie, lilac tortie or chocolate tortie shading or tipping.

Coat: Short, soft and fine in texture.

Body: Medium length, muscular with a straight back. The legs are of medium length, with the hind legs being slightly longer. The paws are oval.

Tail: Medium length to long, carried up and tapering slightly along its length to a rounded tip.

Head: Slightly rounded over the skull, and relatively broad between the ears, which have rounded tips and are well spaced, resembling a butterfly's wings from the front. Short wedge with an evident stop, with a firm chin and even bite.

Eyes: Well spaced and slightly oriental, being green or bluish-green in color, but neither rounded nor almond-shaped.

Life expectancy: 12-15 years.

Black-tipped Burmilla. Tipping should be both symmetrical and even.

SHOW STANDARD

Burmillas with coats that are too long, or those that have a woolly undercoat, will be penalized. Variable tabby markings are typically evident on the legs and tail, with an M-shaped silhouette on the forehead.

California Spangled

The creation of a California-based scriptwriter called Paul Casey, this breed was developed not for show purposes, but specifically to raise awareness about the plight of wild cats, a number of which are under threat of extinction. He planned a careful breeding program to produce a domestic cat with the physique of a wild cat.

KITTENS

Snow Leopards differ from other varieties in that they are white at birth, and it is likely to take up to eighteen months for them to develop their characteristic patterning. Contrast between the spotted patterning and the coat color is very evident in young kittens of other varieties.

Gold. Stripes are always present on the neck, but the back and sides must be spotted.

PROs

- Unique appearance
- Individual patterning
- Easy to look after
- Sound temperament
- Gets along well with dogs and children

CONs

- Difficult to obtain
- Expensive
- Very active by nature
- Not widely shown
- Hard to establish a breeding line

Silver. Good contrast between the black spots and coat is vital.

BREED PROFILE

Basic type: Shorthaired and smooth-coated. A medium-sized cat with an athletic physique.
Size: Medium.
Colors: Exists only in a spotted form. Varieties include gold, silver, charcoal, brown, and blue, all with darker spots. Snow Leopards recognizable by their blue eyes.
Coat: Short and soft in texture. Sleek, especially over the back, but with the fur on the underparts and the tail being slightly longer.
Body: Most characteristic feature is the breed's long, muscular body, which resembles that of a wild cat. The legs are long and angular, emphasizing its lithe movement.
Tail: Tail is of medium length, and is of a consistent diameter, ending in a round tip.
Head: Medium-sized, with a well-developed muzzle and prominent cheekbones. The ears are set high, and have rounded tips.
Eyes: Widely spaced, almond-shaped, with coloration depending on the variety.
Life expectancy: 12-15 years.

SHOW STANDARD

A wide variety of domestic cats, ranging from pure breeds such as Manx and Persians to street cats found in Egypt, contributed to the California Spangled's ancestry, but no wild cats, ensuring it has a very sound temperament. Flaws may include an over-long coat, a tail that tapers, or blotched rather than spotted markings.

Chartreux

This ancient breed has been linked for centuries with the Carthusian monastery of La Grande Chartreuse, which is located near Grenoble, southeast France. It nearly died out in the 1920s, but cross-breeding, especially with Blue British Shorthairs, boosted its numbers. Today, Chartreux are most likely to be seen at shows in France and Belgium.

KITTENS
It is quite common for kittens of this breed to show slight traces of tabby patterning. These so-called "ghost markings" should disappear with age. Their eyes are blue initially, then become brownish-gray before changing to their distinctive orangish shade.

The Chartreux is a stocky breed.

PROs
- Distinctive appearance
- Interesting origins
- Very social cats
- Quiet by nature
- Healthy and easy to look after

CONs
- Not readily obtainable
- Not commonly exhibited
- Stunning eye coloration fades with age
- Mature males develop jowls, affecting their facial shape
- Not a breed that likes to be left alone for long

BREED PROFILE

Basic type: Shorthaired. A relatively large, powerfully built breed.

Size: Medium to large.

Colors: The Chartreux is distinguished partly by its distinctive blue fur. It varies quite widely in its depth of coloration, however, from an ash shade, which is most commonly seen, through to a slate-gray. Silvery tipping, especially around the nose, the whiskers, the back of the ears and the paws, creates an attractive sheen.

Coat: The breed also has a particularly distinctive double coat, which is plush and soft, standing away from the body rather than lying flat. This is the result of its rather woolly undercoat.

Body: A strong cat, with a cobby appearance.

Tail: Medium in length, and will reach as far forwards up the back as the shoulder blades. Tapers along its length to a round tip.

Head: Very distinctive, resembling an inverted trapezium in shape, being slightly longer than it is wide. The ears are set high, creating an impression of alertness.

Eyes: Amber to golden-copper, with the outer corners curving upwards.

Life expectancy: 12-15 years.

SHOW STANDARD

The eyes should not be too rounded, and the appearance of the fur must reflect the resilience of the undercoat. There should be no tendency to lose the breed's key distinctive features, such as the shape of the head, either, which separates it from a British Shorthair.

Its coat coloration and texture are highly distinctive.

Cornish Rex

Few breeds are more instinctively playful than the Cornish Rex. These cats will thrive in an indoor environment, especially if there are a climbing frame and other toys available. The distinctive wavy pattern of their fur is especially apparent over the back.

KITTENS

They are usually born with very wavy coats, but then this characteristic becomes less apparent for a time, once they are about five weeks old. There may be some variance in color at this age as well, depending on the variety. Tortoiseshell Cornish Rexes may have grayish rather than black hairs at first.

Chocolate and White Bicolor. No set pattern of markings is required.

PROs

- Sheds little fur
- Minimal grooming needs
- Forms a strong bond with people
- Gets along well with most dogs
- Placid nature

CONs

- Unhappy outside in cold or wet weather
- Very hearty appetite
- Keen on climbing
- Needs plenty of company
- Show preparation often time-consuming

BREED PROFILE

Basic type: Shorthaired, curly-coated. A relatively long-legged breed with a muscular body and an arched back.

Size: Small to medium.

Colors: There are no restrictions on coloration in the case of the Cornish Rex, although white and dark-colored individuals are both quite common. Those with pointed markings are referred to as Si-Rexes.

Coat: Short, with a dense, wavy appearance and very soft texture. This breed lacks the long, coarse guard hairs, which helps to explain the texture of its coat. Even the whiskers and eyebrows are crinkled.

Body: Slender, muscular and hard, and of medium length. Straight, long legs end in dainty, oval paws.

Tail: Long, tapers along its length and should have a good covering of curly fur.

Head: Length of the head is about a third longer than its width, with a flat top to the skull, and the forehead extends in a straight line down to the nostrils.

Eyes: Medium in size and oval in shape. Color is variable, being blue in the case of Si-Rex varieties.

Life expectancy: 12-15 years.

SHOW STANDARD

The appearance of the coat is vital. It must not show any signs of being shaggy, or excessively short, with bald areas being considered a serious fault, especially in older cats. White markings are deemed a serious flaw in Si-Rexes. The tail must be straight.

The Cornish Rex has a relatively tall but slender body.

69

Cornish Rex

Origins

There has been a tendency to name rex breeds after the part of the world where they first arose, with all such breeds being the result of natural mutations. This particular example originates from the southwestern county of Cornwall in England, and is now one of the most popular. The first kitten of this type cropped up in a litter of farm cats in 1950, and was called Kallibunker.

Changes in Appearance

The rather unusual appearance of these cats meant that they were not instantly popular in England. There they were crossed with British Shorthairs as well as Burmese, which gave them a relatively cobby appearance. The Cornish Rex was first taken to the United States in 1957, at an early stage in its development. This led to a subsequent divergence in type, because in North America Siamese were used as outcrosses for Cornish Rexes, and this created a more elegant and fine-boned appearance that is favored today. As a result, British breeders imported Kallibunker's descendants back to Europe. Every Cornish Rex in existence traces its origins back to this particular individual cat.

A Lilac Point Si-Rex. Body shading may be present on the back and flanks.

The German Angle

Prior to the breeding of Kallibunker, a separate strain of rex cat (so-called because of a similar mutation previously recorded in rabbits) had been recorded in Germany. These particular rexes were different in appearance to the Cornish Rex, having more rounded faces, but genetic studies revealed they were actually caused by the same mutation, which had arisen twice in separate localities. Today, however, while the Cornish Rex is very popular internationally, its German counterpart has since become virtually extinct.

Two calicos, displaying their individual tortoiseshell and white coloration.

Devon Rex

These mischievous-looking cats live up to their appearance. The Devon Rex is one of the most inquisitive of all breeds. They usually form a strong rapport with their owners, proving to be rather dog-like in the way that they will often chase after a toy ball rolled across the floor and bring it back to you.

A Devon Rex tabby kitten.

KITTENS

Young Devon Rexes tend to be born with wavy coats, but may then lose much of their coat for a period. It is very difficult therefore to assess their show potential until they have a full coat at about eighteen months old. The actual appearance of kittens with patterning, though, such as Bicolor forms, will not change with age.

PROs

- A cat of real character
- The most common of the rex breeds
- Bred in a wide color range
- Highly affectionate
- Very little grooming needed

CONs

- May be difficult to locate a particular variety
- Hard to assess a kitten's show potential
- Not hardy
- Coats may appear scruffy at times
- Wide ears may require regular cleaning

BREED PROFILE

Basic type: Shorthaired and curly-coated. A relatively small cat with a slender but muscular appearance.

Size: Small.

Colors: There are no restrictions imposed as far as coloration is concerned in this breed, and once again Si-Rexes, representing a Colorpoint strain, have been created.

Coat: Fine and very short, often creating the impression of waves rippling over the cat's body. Both the eyebrows and whiskers are shorter than normal, with these hairs breaking easily.

Body: Slim yet broad-chested, creating a muscular impression in spite of the breed's relatively small overall size.

Tail: Long and fine, emphasizing the breed's slender shape. Tapers to a point and must be well-covered with hair.

Head: Wedge-shaped, with full cheeks and a short muzzle. The top of the head is flat, while there is a distinct nose break evident between the eyes.

Eyes: These are widely spaced, large and oval in shape, sloping in the direction of the outer edges of the ears. Their coloration is linked to that of the variety concerned.

Life expectancy: 13-15 years.

SHOW STANDARD

A cobby body is heavily penalized, as is a tail that is too short or kinked. The ears must be large, with wide bases and set low, contributing significantly to the Devon Rex's unique appearance. Any deviation from the desired pixie-like head is considered a serious flaw.

The Red Silver form of the Devon Rex.

Devon Rex

Origins

Strangely, the Devon Rex arose in the English county of Devon, which is adjacent to the home of the Cornish Rex, although these breeds are completely unrelated to each other. Close study has revealed that their coat types are very different. In the case of the Devon Rex, all three hair types are present, but the longer guard hairs have become so short that they effectively merge in with the down. The first kitten of this type was recorded in a litter of non-pedigree cats in 1960, and the breed has since become well known internationally.

Black Smoke showing the contrast in its coat.

Bran Baths

Rather than washing their cats before a show, breeders frequently give these rexes a bran bath, so as not to affect the wavy nature of the coat, as will happen temporarily if it is shampooed. A bran bath can be a messy operation, though. The bran, available from pet stores, needs to be warmed up in the oven, and then is massaged thoroughly into the cat's coat, absorbing grease, before being brushed out again. Routine grooming simply entails stroking your cat, although rubbing the hair gently with a piece of silk also helps to impart a healthy gloss.

Temporary Hair Loss

The coat is a very important feature of the Devon Rex, and in some cases there can be bald patches evident, which are regarded as a particularly serious flaw in adult cats. When they are molting, however, these cats may develop temporary bald patches, because of the way in which they shed their fur.

The distinctive wedge-shaped head of this Si-Rex is obvious here. Note the blue eyes in this case.

Egyptian Mau

This breed originates from Cairo, being descended from street cats obtained there in the 1950s. It is thought to be very similar in appearance to the earliest form of the domestic cat. Unfortunately, it is rare, but a separate breed with a very similar appearance is the Oriental Spotted Tabby.

In the Silver, this ground color is very evident in the throat area.

KITTENS

The characteristic spotted patterning is present in young Egyptian Maus from birth, but is usually less distinct at this stage and may be darker. In the case of the Smoke, it can take up to two years for this variety to develop its full coloration. The eye coloration of kittens changes from blue through gray to green, with an amber hue often present until they are about eighteen months old.

PROs

- A particularly striking breed
- Not noisy by nature
- Gets along well with other Egyptian Maus
- Very responsive
- Highly affectionate

CONs

- Often difficult to obtain
- Shy with visitors
- Eye coloration becomes paler with age
- Less social with other cats
- Spotted pattern fades during the molt

BREED PROFILE
Basic type: Shorthaired, smooth-coated. Medium-sized and yet muscular
Size: Medium.
Colors: There are four traditional varieties—pewter, silver, bronze, and smoke.
Coat: Glossy with a silky texture. Distinctive spotted patterning, with the spots being round in shape.
Body: Intermediate type, neither tending towards an Oriental nor a cobby type. The legs are fine and cause the breed to look relatively tall. As the hind legs are long, so the back is inclined to rise slightly in the direction of the hips.
Tail: Relatively long, with a rounded tip.
Head: Wedge-shaped and slightly rounded. The ears are broad and quite large, with rounded tips. The nose is straight, with no stop.
Eyes: Almond-shaped upper lids contrast with the rounded shape of the lower lids. Coloration is gooseberry-green.
Life expectancy: 12-14 years.

SHOW STANDARD
The spots should not overlap, giving rise to blotches or barring, but must be discrete. The body type of these cats must not be too cobby either, while the tail must be straight and free from a kink anywhere along its length.

Bronze—aside from the spots, there is black ticking to the individual hairs.

Exotic

Few cats have a more appealing appearance than the Exotic. It closely resembles its Persian relative in terms of its physical appearance or "type," while at the same time its coat is much more easily kept in top condition.

Cream Exotic— a variety susceptible to unwanted tabby markings.

KITTENS

The coats of Exotic kittens often resemble those of young Persian Longhairs at first, but the difference in coat length soon becomes clearly apparent within the first few weeks. Some "self" varieties, particularly cream and red individuals, may display "ghost markings" in the form of slight tabby barring, but these should fade. In terms of their temperament, Exotic kittens are less lively than many other breeds.

PROs

- Very cuddly appearance
- Extremely relaxed temperament
- Quiet by nature
- Available in a wide range of color varieties
- Easy-care coat

CONs

- Compact face shape increases risk of tear-staining
- May be noisy sleepers
- Can shed quite heavily
- Not especially active by nature
- May be bullied by more assertive cats

BREED PROFILE

Basic type: Medium-length coat, stocky build, and relatively large in size.

Size: Large.

Colors: All of the colors that are currently recognized in the case of the Persian Longhair are acceptable in this breed. This includes self colors such as blue and cream, bicolors, smoke and tipped varieties, tabbies, and tortoiseshell variants.

Coat: Dense, plush and soft, with its density preventing it from lying flat. It is longer than that of other shorthairs.

Body: Cobby overall, deep-chested and with thick, short, straight forelegs. The back is level.

Tail: Short and thick with a blunt tip.

Head: Large, flat and rounded in shape, with powerful jaws and full cheeks. The nose is short and stubby, displaying an evident stop. The small ears are low-set, in such a way as not to break the rounded impression created by the face. They tilt slightly forwards, giving the cat a lively appearance.

Eyes: Well spaced, round and large, with their color corresponding to that of the coat.

Life expectancy: 12-15 years.

SHOW STANDARD

Beware of unwanted flecks of color in the eyes or a rim of a different color, such as green in the case of an Orange-eyed White, which can crop up occasionally. Any signs of contrasting white hair on the chest of "self" individuals will be regarded as a serious flaw, as will an uneven ground color in tabbies.

The relatively flat face of the Exotic is a feature of its Persian ancestry.

Exotic

Origins

As had occurred previously in Britain, where crosses between the British Shorthair and Persians had been carried out repeatedly to increase the size of the shorthaired breed, a similar breeding policy was followed in North America during the development of the American Shorthair. However, some of the resulting shorthaired offspring more closely resembled Persians in their type than the American Shorthair, and it was from these that the Exotic was created in the 1950s, although the breed was not actually recognized under this name until 1966. The description "Exotic" was chosen because it signified the fact that one of the breed's ancestors came from overseas.

A corresponding breeding program of this type was then followed in Britain to create a very similar type of cat, also known as the Exotic, although in this case British rather than American Shorthairs were used.

Grooming

One of the great attractions of the Exotic is that its grooming needs are quite minimal, in comparison with Persians, but be prepared for heavy shedding of the dense undercoat in the spring. These cats are potentially then more at risk from hairballs than other shorthaired breeds, especially at this stage. They may therefore benefit from a food containing ingredients that actually help to prevent the formation of these pads of molted hair in the stomach in the first place.

Red Tabby—the shorter coat compared with a Persian emphasizes the tabby patterning.

Creating More Varieties

As the range of varieties has continued to expand in the case of the Persian, so has the number in the case of the Exotic breed, because outcrossings to Persians are still permitted. This means that developing new colors or patterns is quite easy, enhancing the appeal of the Exotic to breeders as a result.

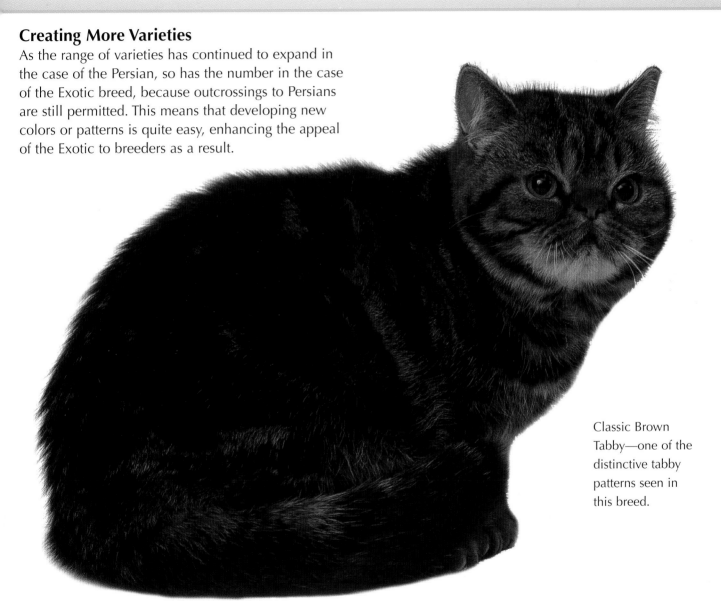

Classic Brown Tabby—one of the distinctive tabby patterns seen in this breed.

Japanese Bobtail

This unusual breed has been kept in Japan for over 1,000 years, where it was originally the property of the nobility. Faced with a plague of rodents in the 1600s, however, the authorities decided to allow anyone to own one. The Japanese Bobtail has since become known as *Kazoku Neko*, which translates as the family cat of Japan, reflecting the fact that it is now a much-loved companion.

The Japanese Bobtail's short tail has been likened to a pom-pom.

KITTENS

All young Japanese Bobtails have blue eyes at first, changing gradually to their adult appearance. There may also be faint smudges on the coat, notably on the head of Whites, and these may not disappear until after the cats are perhaps a year old.

PROs

- A cat with great personality
- Relates very well to people
- Lives in harmony with dogs and other cats
- Individual and attractive patterning
- Does not molt heavily

CONs

- Not especially numerous outside Japan
- Blue eyes in adults may be linked with deafness
- Shortened tail may not appeal
- Natural curiosity can lead these cats into danger
- Lack of competitive showing opportunities

BREED PROFILE

Basic type: Shorthaired, relatively smooth coat with a tall yet slender and muscular appearance.

Size: Medium.

Colors: Traditional variety is the *mi-ke*, which is a combination of red, black and white. Other varieties include bicolors, in red or black and white, as well as tortoiseshell, and self colors in white, red and black.

Coat: Short, with the coat lying quite flat, and lacking any significant undercoat.

Body: Narrow, long body with an athletic build.

Tail: A very short tail, kinked or curved in appearance, which should not exceed four inches in length.

Head: Wedge-shaped, with high cheekbones, and tall ears that are located at the corners of the face.

Eyes: Any eye color is permitted, and odd-eyed individuals, with blue and orange eyes, also occur, with the eyes themselves being slanted.

Life expectancy: 12-15 years.

These cats often display predominantly white areas on their coats.

SHOW STANDARD

No cross-breeding with other cats is permitted, but the semi-long Japanese Bobtails, which are rarer, may be mated with shorthairs and occur in their litters too. The tortoiseshell varieties are essentially female-only, for genetic reasons, and this can complicate the breeding of these cats.

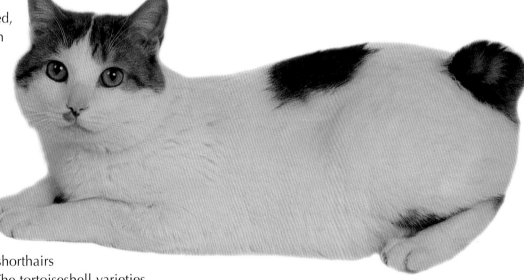

Korat

This is a breed that is traditionally said to bestow good fortune on its owner. For centuries in this cat's Thai homeland, Korats have been given as gifts to couples on their wedding day, but they were unknown in the West until the late 1800s, and their exact origins are obscure.

KITTENS

Their eyes change from blue through amber to green, but this is a slow process that may take up to two years or even longer in some cases. Their coat coloration can also be equally slow to develop, over the course of successive molts.

The Korat's coat has an unusual silvery sheen.

PROs

- Appealing appearance
- Very straightforward coat care
- Happy in hot climates
- Very affectionate
- Inquisitive nature

CONs

- Can display signs of jealousy
- Vocal, although its calls are unusually melodious
- Enjoys climbing
- Restricted availability
- Slow to attain adult coloration

BREED PROFILE

Basic type: Shorthaired, smooth-coated. A medium-sized cat, with males being larger and more muscular than females, which have a more dainty appearance overall.

Size: Medium.

Colors: Blue in color, which can vary quite significantly in its shade, with silver tipping that should be as extensive on the individual hairs as possible. Recently both lilac and chocolate cats with a similar appearance to Korats have emerged in some bloodlines. These are not recognized as true Korats, but are described as being of Korat type.

Coat: Glossy, lies flat on the body as there is no undercoat, with the hair being short to medium in length.

Korats are named after a northern Thai province.

Body: Intermediate between the very svelte appearance of Siamese and the cobby profile of breeds such as the British Shorthair. Legs are in proportion to the body, with the paws being oval.

Tail: Medium length, tapers to a rounded tip.

Head: Very distinctive, heart-shaped face, with large ears set high on the head.

Eyes: Brilliant green.

Life expectancy: 12-15 years.

SHOW STANDARD

There should be no hint of tabby markings in the coat, with great emphasis being placed on the Korat's color, as far as judging is concerned. The tail must not be kinked in any way.

Manx

The Manx is one of the best-known breeds in the world, thanks to its lack of a tail. As a result, many people assume that all Manx are tail-less, but in fact there are actually far more Manx kittens born with tails, to the extent that Manx cats without tails are very rare.

Blue Manx. Kittens may show slight tabby markings at first.

KITTENS
Young Manx kittens are identical to adults, although at first their eye coloration will be blue in all cases. It is possible to recognize tail-less individuals at birth, compared with those that have tails. The Manx is not a prolific breed, however, and litter sizes are small, usually averaging just three kittens.

PROs

- Very long-lived
- Highly unusual and distinctive
- Placid, friendly nature
- Gets along very well with dogs
- Playful nature

CONs

- Difficult to acquire
- Self-colored Manx not especially common
- Can become one-person cats
- Less elegant than other cats when moving
- Genetic concerns over breeding

BREED PROFILE

Basic type: Shorthaired. Medium in size, with a powerful, compact build.

Size: Medium

Colors: There are no restrictions on color in the case of the Manx, although in some cases Manx with Siamese-type markings are not recognized, as these are not traditionally associated with the breed.

Coat: This is in the form of a distinctive double layer, with a relatively coarse, open top coat combined with a short but very dense undercoat.

Body: Strong, and curved, with a rounded appearance, thanks to the short back and rounded hindquarters, which are higher than the shoulders. The flanks are very deep.

Tail: In exhibition Manx, no tail is present, although these cats can have tails.

Head: Large and rounded, with prominent cheeks and muzzle. The ears are large, set high on the head, and angled outwards, tapering to a rounded tip, and are angled slightly outwards.

Eyes: Round and large, corresponding in color to that of the coat.

Life expectancy: 14-18 years.

SHOW STANDARD

It is vital that there is not even the hint of a tail that could interfere with the smooth profile of the rump. The texture of the coat is a vital feature, with very little emphasis being placed on the coloration or markings of these cats during judging.

Cream and White is the palest bicolor combination. The depth of cream coloration can vary significantly.

Manx

Origins

The Manx is named after the Isle of Man, off England's northwestern coast, where it is believed to have originated. There are various stories that have evolved to explain the tail-less nature of these cats. Some suggest that they are descended from cats washed ashore from Spanish galleons wrecked off the coast after the Spanish Armada of 1588. In truth, however, the breed probably arose as the result of a genetic mutation that occurred naturally in the cat population on the island centuries ago. Manx were well-represented at the early cat shows held in Britain in the late 1800s, and in the United States they were one of the first breeds to be recognized for show purposes, being first exhibited there in 1933.

Black and White. Bicolors are common in the case of the Manx.

Tail-less or not?

There are four distinct divisions of Manx cat. Those seen at shows are known as Rumpies, because of their rounded hindquarters and the total absence of a tail. In contrast, the Rumpy-risers have just the trace of a tail, whereas Stumpies have a longer, slightly movable tail. Finally, there are Longies, so-called because their tail is very similar to that of other cats in appearance.

Breeding

A Rumpy Manx has to be mated with one of the other variants, and not with another Rumpy, because there is a lethal genetic factor associated with such pairings, which means that some of the kittens will die before birth. Longhaired Manx sometimes crop up in litters—they are now known as Cymrics. The Manx mutation actually affects the whole of the vertebral column, and not just the tail, and this explains why the back of these cats slopes, and also why they have an unusual hopping gait not seen in other cats.

Cream Tabby and White. The markings are highly individual.

Munchkin

There is no mistaking the controversial Munchkin breed, with its characteristic short-legged appearance. A number of breeders expressed great alarm about the health of these cats at the outset, but it now appears that these fears may have been somewhat misplaced. The breed today generally seems to be quite sound.

Munchkin Colorpoint variants are not uncommon today.

KITTENS

These are similar to adults in appearance, although all varieties have blue eyes at first. In common with other similar breed varieties, Colorpointed Munchkins are white at birth, and then gradually develop the distinctive coloring of their points, on the face, ears, legs, paws and tail.

PROs

- Playful, affectionate nature
- Very distinctive appearance
- Cannot jump onto work tops
- Minimal grooming
- Gets along well with dogs

CONs

- Short legs not universally appealing
- Lacks the natural athleticism of other cats
- Still scarce outside North America
- Can slip under furniture easily
- May have difficulty grooming itself

BREED PROFILE

Basic type: Shorthaired, with a relatively smooth coat. Medium-length body with distinctive short legs.
Size: Medium.
Colors: There are no restrictions on the Munchkin's coloration or patterning.

Although the early examples often reflected their non-pedigree origins, frequently being tabbies of various types, today's examples include colorpoints and "selfs."
Coat: Short, relatively dense and with a typical crisp texture.
Body: Medium in size, with a broad, deep chest. The legs are straight and muscular and noticeably shortened, compared with those of other cats. The front legs may measure no more than three inches overall, with the hind legs being only slightly longer.
Tail: Medium length, tapering slightly along its length.
Head: Medium-sized and slightly wedge-shaped, with the ears being relatively large and rounded at their tips.
Eyes: Large and walnut-shaped, slanting slightly down towards the nose.
Life expectancy: 13-15 years.

SHOW STANDARD

Great emphasis has been placed on ensuring soundness in the case of the Munchkin. Any signs of twisting of the legs, with paws being turned in or out rather than held straight, or of the hocks of the hind legs pointing in towards each other will result in such cats being disqualified. The same applies in the case of any indication of back weakness.

Origins

All of today's Munchkins are descended from a stray cat of this type that was found in Louisiana in 1983. Christened Blackberry, she produced some similar kittens when she bred in due course. The gene responsible for their short-legged appearance is dominant. This means that if a Munchkin is mated with a cat with legs of normal length, then on average half of the resulting kittens should have short legs. This has meant that it has been quite easy to transfer new colors and patterns into Munchkin bloodlines. The breed has been exhibited in the United States since 1995.

Ocicat

This attractively spotted tabby breed came about by chance in 1964, from an unplanned mating in the United States between two Siamese, one of which had a part-Abyssinian ancestry, so they became known for a time as Accicats. Their striking spotted patterning resembles that of a New World wild cat called the Ocelot, however, and so these names were finally combined together, creating the description of Ocicat.

Lavender Silver. This variety has a paler silvery undercoat compared with the Lavender itself.

KITTENS

All young Ocicats have blue eyes at first, which will change gradually in color. Their coats tend to be darker at this stage, lightening with age, and their spotted patterning will become more clearly defined in due course as well.

PROs

- Stunning wild-type patterning
- Docile nature
- Not very noisy
- Easy to groom
- Thrives on attention

CONs

- Large size, weighing up to 15lb
- Correspondingly hearty appetite
- Eye color may fade with age
- Demanding patterning for show purposes
- Separate European strain

BREED PROFILE

Basic type: Shorthaired, smooth-coated. A relatively large and muscular cat, yet elegant and graceful in its movements.

Size: Large.

Colors: These include tawny (which is brown in color), as well as chocolate, cinnamon, blue, lavender, and fawn, plus silver varieties of these colors, all displaying the characteristic spotted patterning, which must be well-defined.

Coat: Relatively short, with a fine texture, and yet long enough to show distinctive ticked tabby banding on the individual hairs.

Body: Large in size but intermediate in type, between the extreme svelte profile of Oriental breeds and the cobby appearance of the American Shorthair.

Tail: Relatively long compared with the length of the body, and tapers to a point.

Head: Intermediate wedge-shaped, with the ears merging into the outside of the cheeks, being broad at the base.

Eyes: Almond-shaped, quite widely spaced. Often amber or green. Must not be blue in color.

Life expectancy: 12-14 years.

SHOW STANDARD

The spots must not overlap each other—this is regarded as a serious flaw. They may fade temporarily during the molt. Kittens without the spotted patterning that are born in litters of Ocicats will be registered as Any Other Variety.

Silver Spotted kitten, with typical tabby markings on the head.

Oriental

The number of Oriental varieties has expanded dramatically over recent years, and these cats have also become very popular as pets, in addition to being seen frequently on the show bench. The choice that now exists does mean, however, that you may have to be patient to obtain one of the more unusual color combinations.

Havana and Lavender. Two of the earliest Oriental Shorthair varieties.

KITTENS

All are born with blue eyes, although this color generally changes first to gray, then grayish-green, and finally to green. The markings of young spotted tabbies may also alter with age, with the spots on the back of kittens forming a solid line that breaks down into spots.

PROs

- Cats of real elegance and beauty
- Highly affectionate
- Very wide range of varieties
- Easy grooming
- Well-suited to family life

CONs

- May be rather vulnerable to respiratory infections
- Sexually precocious, can be mature at four months old
- Noisy by nature
- Capable of learning how to open fridges
- May persistently demand attention

BREED PROFILE

Basic type: Shorthaired, smooth-coated. A svelte, long-bodied breed with a very elegant appearance.
Size: Medium.
Colors: A huge range including "selfs," bicolors, tortoiseshells, tabbies, silvers, smokes, shaded and tipped varieties. It has been calculated that there are now in excess of 400 different possible combinations.
Coat: Fine and silky in texture, short and very sleek, as well as being glossy in appearance.
Body: Long, slender neck with a similar body and a tight abdomen. The legs too are long and slim, with the hind legs being longer than the front legs. The paws are small and oval in shape.
Tail: Continues the line of the body, being long and tapering along its length.
Head: Wedge-shaped head, being not round or pointed in appearance. The long shape of the head starts off being broad between the eyes, and narrows to the fine muzzle. The long nose is straight, without any stop. The ears are large and wide at their bases, effectively extending the lines of the wedge by their positioning, emphasizing the triangular shape of the face.
Eyes: Well spaced, almond-shaped, usually green in color and sloping towards the nose.
Life expectancy: 12-14 years.

Black. Also known as the Ebony because of its appearance.

SHOW STANDARD

There must be no kinking of the tail, and the state of the coat is very important. This should not be long or display any tendency towards coarseness. There must also be no pronounced cheek muscles, which would destroy the straight lines of the face. Any flecks of unwanted contrasting colors in the eyes are a serious flaw.

Oriental

Origins

In the early days after the introduction of Siamese to the West during the late 1800s there was both a colorpointed, blue-eyed strain and a related group of green-eyed cats that occurred in a wide range of solid colors and patterns. Ultimately, by the 1920s however, this green-eyed bloodline had died out, being no longer recognized for show purposes.

Then in 1952, a breeder in England was seeking to breed Colorpoint Longhairs, and as part of this program she crossed a Seal Point Siamese tom with a cross-bred black shorthair that was part Black Persian and part Siamese. Among the kittens was a chocolate brown kitten, which was originally called Havana because its coloration was said to resemble that of a Havana cigar. Subsequently, this description was changed to Chestnut Brown for a period up until 1970, when there was overwhelming support for reverting to its original name.

Meanwhile, in 1956, Havana kittens were sent to a breeder in California, laying the foundation for the breed in North America. A difference in type has since arisen, because whereas in Britain the Havana was developed to be a solid-colored cat with the type of a Siamese, the breeding program in North America has prohibited the use of Siamese outcrosses, so that these cats have slightly more rounded, less angular faces today.

Red. A variety that may show hints of tabby markings, even when adult.

Subsequent Developments

The creation of the Havana led to the creation of a range of other solid-colored cats of this variety. Among the first was the Lavender, known in the UK as Lilac. In the early days, these colors were also often called Foreign, to describe their type. Today, however, this description has been dropped from all such varieties in the UK, apart from the Foreign White, whose breeders preferred to retain the original name of these cats. In the United States, however, these cats have always been known as Oriental Shorthairs.

Blue. Note how the eyes slope down to the nose in this breed.

Oriental

How Orientals Were Created

The aim of breeders was to transfer different colors and patterns into Oriental bloodlines, without having a long-term impact on the characteristic appearance of these cats. As an example, the Cinnamon was first bred during the 1960s in the Netherlands by crossings between Havanas and Sorrel Abyssinians, to introduce the desired coloring. This in turn paved the way for the creation of the Fawn in a similar way, with subsequent refinements being made with new varieties to improve their type after the initial crossings.

The Start of the Revival

The first Oriental variety to be created was actually not the Havana, but rather the black form now described as Ebony, although initially such cats were ignored. They were created by matings between Siamese and Russian Blues, but strangely, however, these cats were overlooked as a variety right up until the 1980s, when they finally came to prominence. A very sleek, black coat is an essential feature—there must be no rusty hue or odd white hairs in the coats of these Orientals.

Silver Smoke. The coloration of these cats is most apparent when they move.

Tabby Strains

These were created by using Lynx (Tabby) Pointed Siamese. Today, all four tabby patterns are well established in the case of the Oriental. The short, sleek coats of these cats are ideal for displaying the clarity of tabby patterning with unrivalled intensity. In the case of Spotted Tabbies, the spotted markings should stand out very clearly, while Ticked Tabbies have bodies free from the usual solid tabby markings, with bands of ticking on their hairs instead. There are likely to be two or three alternating bands of dark and light areas on each hair.

As with other tabby varieties, however, Oriental Ticked Tabbies still display the M-shaped tabby mark on the head, as well as the rings (called necklaces) around the upper chest, with striping on the legs and tail, which ends in a dark tip. This particular tabby has proved to be a very popular variant in the case of the Oriental breed, with the ticked patterning helping to emphasize the characteristic body shape.

Classic Oriental Tabbies display the very evident so-called oyster mark on their flanks, which has led to them also being known as Blotched Tabbies. Their tabby markings are more extensive, compared with other varieties. The patterning of Mackerel Orientals consists of relatively thin vertical lines extending down the sides of the flanks, although this would seem to be the least popular Oriental tabby variant.

Caramel Silver Ticked Tabby. One of the many composite Oriental Shorthair varieties that have been created.

Oriental

A Chance Encounter

Not all of today's Oriental varieties were created deliberately. In 1970, a chance mating between a Silver Chinchilla Persian and a Siamese saw the emergence of the Oriental Shaded group. They include the Oriental Tipped varieties as well, which are basically identical to the Shaded, but are paler in color because the dark tipping at the ends of their hairs is not as extensive as in their Shaded counterparts.

This breeding program also led to the emergence of the Oriental Smoke. The undercoat in this case is white, similarly the base of the guard hairs, with the tips of being blackish, creating an impression of smoke as the cat moves. A brand new "self" color was also developed from this bloodline, which is now known as the Caramel. These cats are a bluish fawn in color and, as in other "self" varieties, the nose, as well as the paw pads and even the eye rims, are similarly colored. This is not to be confused with the much browner Cinnamon variety, which was known for a period in the United States under the same name.

Chocolate Spotted Tabby. The spots must be round, but can vary in size.

Changes with age

Unlike their Siamese relatives, the body coloration of Orientals does not alter as adult cats grow older. Their eye coloration is likely to fade, however, and freckles of darker pigmentation often appear on the nose, ears, lips, and eye rims of paler varieties such as the Cream and Red. These may even extend to the paws, although they will be less obvious here. Mild speckling of this type is not held against a cat on the show bench, but the coloration itself, in the case of these "self" varieties, must remain consistent to the roots.

Chocolate Ticked Tabby. Darker patterning such as chocolate highlights are seen in this variety's patterning.

Oriental

Parti-colors

Cats displaying white and colored areas of fur have existed in Oriental bloodlines for many years, and represent a further area for future expansion. In these cases, the white and colored areas must be well defined, with no overlapping of white hairs in the colored areas of the coat. Various calico forms, displaying tortoiseshell and white coloration, are also possible.

Tortoiseshells

The range of tortoiseshell varieties in the case of the Oriental is also very large, reflecting the wide range of "self" colors that exist in the breed. Creation of these colors has not required further outcrossing to other breeds, but simply the use of the "self" variety itself. As a result, the range of tortoiseshell colors includes Oriental Caramel Torties and Oriental Fawn Torties, with these cats likely to be almost exclusively female for genetic reasons.

Silver Spotted Tabby. The contrast between the markings and coat color are pronounced.

Coat considerations

The various crossings that have expanded the Oriental group so dramatically over recent years, and particularly the use of Persian Longhairs for this purpose, have resulted in the emergence of odd longhaired kittens in the litters of Oriental shorthairs. Some breeders have sought to develop these cats into a longhaired strain, differing only from their shorthaired cousins in terms of their coat length.

Unfortunately, however, the longer coat length in such cases not only obscures the svelte physique of these cats to an extent, but also it causes the markings to become obscured, simply because the coat is not as sleek. Unsurprisingly therefore, Oriental Longhairs as a group have attained nothing like the popularity of their shorthaired relative.

Chocolate Spotted Tabby. All Orientals are similar in type, irrespective of their coloration.

Russian

First bred in the vicinity of the port of Archangel, on the northern coast of Russia, this breed started to become well known both in North America and the United Kingdom in the 1880s. Quiet by nature, the Russian forms a strong bond with its owner and will make a playful companion.

KITTENS

It is not unusual for blue kittens to have pinkish-lavender pads when young. Russian blacks may have a rusty tinge to their coat at this stage, while whites can display a dark area on the head that should disappear with age.

Mother and kitten. The young cat's coat is likely to become more silver as it matures.

PROs

- Ideal companion for someone living alone
- Placid nature
- Unique fine, silky-textured coat
- Easy to groom
- Likely to get along well with other cats

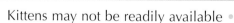

CONs

- Kittens may not be readily available
- Frequently rather wary of visitors
- Not ideal alongside boisterous children
- Queens often do not call loudly in breeding condition
- Vivid green color of the eyes fades with age

BREED PROFILE

Basic type: Shorthaired, with a very distinctive coat texture. Relatively elongated body. The legs are quite long, with the paws being small and dainty, and oval in shape.

Size: Medium.

Colors: Traditionally blue, with a decidedly silvery sheen. Now both a pure black and also a white variety exist, as well as a rarer red form. Its name has therefore been changed from Russian Blue as a consequence.

Coat: Short but double-layered coat that is raised away from the body, with a dense yet silky texture.

Body: Long and quite elegant, with the tail being in proportion to the body and tapering slightly along its length.

Head: Very distinctive wedge-shaped head, with the top of the skull between the ears being flat. The whisker pads are quite prominent in this breed. There is no break in profile from the forehead down to the nose.

Eyes: Almond-shaped, well spaced, and bright green in color.

Life expectancy: 12-14 years.

SHOW STANDARD

Some cross-breeding with Siamese was carried out in the late 1940s, when the breed had become very scarce in the West, but today any indication of a Siamese type or a flat coat are serious flaws, as are any slight tabby markings in adults, or scattered white hairs.

Russians are rather phlegmatic cats by nature.

Savannah

The Savannah is the result of cross-breeding between the African wild cat known as the Serval and domestic cats, which began in the United States during the 1980s. After initial matings with a Serval parent, subsequent generations of kittens became progressively friendlier and smaller, as the result of being mated only with domestic cats.

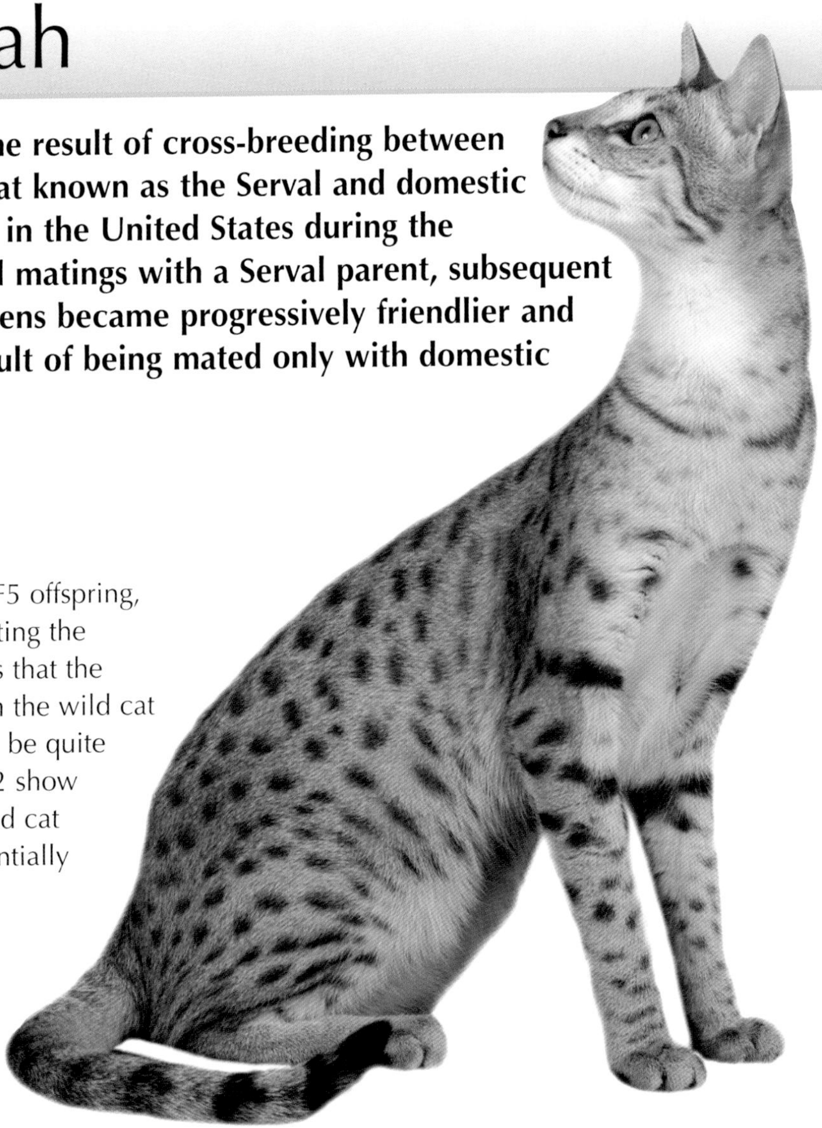

This breed is now the largest of all pet cats.

KITTENS

Ideally, choose F4 or F5 offspring, with this figure indicating the number of generations that the kitten is removed from the wild cat mating. F3 kittens can be quite friendly, but F1 and F2 show distinctive signs of wild cat behavior and are essentially unsuitable as pets.

PROs

- Highly distinctive appearance
- Unique markings
- Wild look with tame personality
- Intelligent nature
- Likes water

CONs

- May not like cuddling
- Keen hunting instincts
- Relatively expensive
- Costly to keep
- Very energetic and lively

BREED PROFILE

Basic type: Relatively shorthaired. Large, long-legged and powerfully built. Females are significantly lighter than males.

Size: Varies, with F1 cats measuring eighteen inches at the shoulder, while F4 Savannahs are more typically fifteen inches tall.

Colors: Usually brown spotted or silver spotted, but black and black smokes are also recognized, and occasionally snow (white-colored) Savannahs occur.

Coat: Short to medium in length, with the outer coat having a slightly coarse texture, compared with the soft undercoat.

Body: Semi-foreign in type, with a very long neck and well-developed, powerful hips and thighs. The legs are slender, long and muscular, with the hind legs being slightly longer than the front legs, while the paws are oval in shape.

Tail: Relatively thick and quite long, tapering to a blunt tip.

Head: Takes the shape of an equilateral triangle, with the head overall being small in comparison with the body. The muzzle tapers and the nostrils are low-set. The ears are large and wide at the base, being set high on the head.

Eyes: Slope downwards in the direction of the nose, being quite deep set and low on the forehead. Should be vivid and rich in color.

Life expectancy: 12-14 years.

SHOW STANDARD

Unsurprisingly, a sound temperament is considered vital, and Savannahs must accept being handled without hesitation. Oriental Shorthairs, Egyptian Maus, and non-pedigrees have been used as outcrosses to shape the breed's appearance.

Savannahs are so-called because of their link with Africa.

Shorthaired Scottish Fold

These unusual cats were developed from a chance mutation, which arose in 1951 on a farm in Scotland. For many years, however, they were banned from being shown in Britain because of misplaced fears that their unusual ear carriage could leave them vulnerable to infections, and their development has taken place largely in North America.

The rounded facial shape of Scottish Folds is very appealing.

KITTENS

At birth, Scottish Fold kittens are indistinguishable in appearance from littermates that have normal ears, as their ears do not start to fold until they are about two to three weeks of age. The eyes are blue in all cases at this stage.

PROs

- Very appealing appearance
- Cuddly disposition
- Placid, tolerant nature
- Grooming straightforward
- Hardy nature

CONs

- Impossible to recognize kittens with folded ears at first
- Careful breeding policy necessary
- Possible leg and tail weaknesses
- White Scottish Folds may be deaf
- Degree of folding differs between individuals

BREED PROFILE

Basic type: Shorthaired, with a compact, rounded, muscular body shape.

Size: Medium.

Colors: There is no restriction on coloration in this breed although, whereas bicolors are commonly seen, colorpointed variants are generally much rarer, and are not universally accepted for show purposes.

Coat: Short and dense, forming a double layer which is resilient, rather than lying sleek against the body.

Body: Thick-set and short, with the legs being stocky and in proportion to the body.

Tail: Medium-length to long, and must be flexible, ideally tapering to a point.

Head: Rounded, with a broad, short nose and relatively wide muzzle and a moderate chin. Mature tom cats have prominent jowls. The ears are set rather in the position of a cap, not high on the head. They must fold forwards and downwards, ideally being both relatively small and tightly folded, with the tips being rounded.

Eyes: Large and round, matching the color of the coat.

Life expectancy: 12-15 years.

Black and White. Bicolor variations of this breed are popular.

SHOW STANDARD

The tail must be flexible, as fusion of the vertebrae can occur in the Scottish Fold. Folds must always be mated with those cats that have normal ear carriage (called Non-folds), to avoid potential weaknesses in the tail and feet in kittens.

Selkirk Rex

All today's Selkirk Rexes trace their ancestry back to a stray kitten, handed into an animal shelter in Wyoming in 1987. Since then, the breed has established a worldwide following. This mutation affects all three layers of hair in the coat, underlying their curly-coated appearance.

A Black Tortoiseshell Selkirk Rex. The patterning is highly individual.

KITTENS

They are born with curly coats, but then these hairs are replaced once they are about six months old. Subsequently, the coat looks sparse and rather wiry for a couple of months, until the young cats then start to grow their adult coat. It can take two years to develop to its fullest extent.

PROs

- Hardy rex breed
- Very affectionate disposition
- Thick coat, unlike some rexes
- Dominant mutation, so easy to breed
- Playful disposition

CONs

- Slow to develop adult coat
- Curliness most evident on the neck and tail
- Coat can look rough at times
- Rarer than Devon or Cornish Rexes
- Climate may affect condition of the coat

A Black Smoke Tortoiseshell Selkirk Rex. Recognizable by its white undercoat.

BREED PROFILE

Basic type: Curly-coated, with a relatively stocky build and yet well proportioned overall.

Size: Medium to large.

Colors: There are no restrictions as far as coloration in this breed is concerned. "Selfs" tend to be less common perhaps, compared with tabbies and torties, reflecting the non-pedigree origin of this breed.

Coat: Medium length, with a soft, plush texture. It takes the form of a double-layered coat, with a wavy top coat and a thick undercoat. Whiskers and eyebrows both curled.

Body: Muscular, relatively large profile with strong legs. Both sexes develop jowls in this case, but females are lighter in build than males.

Tail: Medium in length, relatively thick and with curly fur, tapering to a tip.

Head: Rounded in shape, with a wide forehead. The ears are well spaced and of medium size.

Eyes: Well spaced, large and round in shape.

Life expectancy: 12-15 years.

SHOW STANDARD

A number of breeds have contributed to the subsequent development of the Selkirk Rex, underlying its type. They include both American and British Shorthairs, as well as the Exotic. Just one Selkirk Rex parent should result in further rex kittens, thanks to the dominant nature of this mutation.

Siamese

One of the most recognizable and well known of all cat breeds, the Siamese makes a strong-minded companion. These cats now have much more angular heads than their ancestors seen in the late 1800s, which were brought from the Southeast Asian country of Siam, which is now known as Thailand.

Chocolate Lynx Point. Tabby markings are evident in the colored areas of fur.

KITTENS

Young Siamese are whitish and then develop their characteristic pointed coloration gradually. The signs usually first appear on the tail and ears, with the mask developing later. Their calls will also become far more assertive and louder as they grow older.

PROs

- Exceedingly playful by nature
- Thrive alongside dogs
- Exceedingly affectionate
- Very sociable
- Ideal if you want two cats

CONs

- Very noisy, with a loud voice
- Queens may conceive at just four months
- Agile and avid bird hunters
- Like climbing indoors and out
- Prone to chronic respiratory infections

BREED PROFILE

Basic type: Shorthaired, smooth-coated. A very sleek, fit appearance characterizes these cats.

Size: Medium.

Colors: Seal point, chocolate point, blue point, and lilac point are the traditional colors. Many other varieties now exist, however, including cream and red points, as well as numerous lynx (tabby) and tortie point variants, plus torbie points, displaying both tortie and lynx point coloring.

Coat: Sleek and short, with a glossy texture.

Body: Long and svelte, with an elegant neck, slim legs and small, oval paws. The hind legs are slightly longer than the front legs.

Tail: Long, straight and tapering.

Head: Long and triangular in shape, narrowing down to a fine muzzle, with a straight profile. The ears are large, triangular in shape, and have wide bases.

Eyes: Almond-shaped, bright blue in color and slant down towards the eyes.

Life expectancy: 12-15 years.

SHOW STANDARD

A squint or any kink in the tail are regarded as very serious faults. The show career of these cats tends to be quite limited, because shading develops over their hindquarters, particularly in the case of varieties with darker points, such as the Seal Point. Non-standard varieties are often described as Colorpoint Shorthairs.

Blue Point Siamese. The point coloration is light bluish-gray.

Singapura

This distinctive breed is supposedly descended from a population of homeless cats living around Singapore harbor, five of which were taken to the United States in the 1970s. In spite of their feral roots, Singapuras make excellent companions.

KITTENS

Their coats may appear longer or thicker at first, partly because their bodies are small, and the barring on the legs can be slow to develop, as may their color. Ticking can also be uneven at first in young Singapuras. It takes about nine weeks before their eyes start to change from blue and acquire their adult coloration.

An adult Singapura.

PROs

- Active and curious by nature
- Compact size
- Very easy to care for
- Highly distinctive patterning
- Affectionate, likes being stroked

CONs

- Still a rare breed
- Correspondingly costly
- Show opportunities limited
- Can be quite vocal
- Exists as a single color variety

BREED PROFILE

Basic type: Shorthaired, smooth-coated. A small yet muscular ticked tabby that typically weighs less than 6lb when adult, ranking as the lightest of all pure-breds. Males are larger than females.

Size: Small.

Colors: Only occurs as a Sable Ticked Tabby, with rich sable brown ticking on the upperparts and sides of the body. The ground color is described as "old ivory," having a slightly yellowish hue. Each hair has two bands of dark markings, being light at the roots and dark at the tips. The area from the muzzle down on to the chin and the underparts is pale, being said to resemble unbleached muslin.

Coat: Short, silky in texture and smooth.

Body: Very distinctive, compact profile, supported on strong, muscular legs that become much daintier towards the small, oval-shaped paws.

Tail: Relatively long, can be curled back just short of the level of the shoulder, ending in a blunt tip.

Head: Rounded in shape, with a medium-length muzzle, although adult males develop jowls. The ears are large and wide at the base.

Eyes: Almond-shaped and large, with acceptable coloration being shades of green, gold, copper or hazel.

Life expectancy: 12-15 years.

SHOW STANDARD

Blue eyes are not acceptable. The coat color must not be gray, giving a cold impression. Dark barring should be present only inside and not outside the front legs. The muzzle must not be short.

A young kitten.

Snowshoe

The white areas on the feet help to explain the name of these cats, which were created in the United States in the 1960s. They are not as extreme in type as Siamese, with American Shorthairs having been used in their development, and they are also less demanding by nature.

KITTENS

Young Snowshoes are essentially white at birth, and only develop their coloration slowly. This can take up to two years to develop fully. It is not unusual for signs of faint tabby barring, described as ghost markings, to be present on the coats of kittens, but these should disappear with age.

The brilliant blue eyes of the affectionate Snowshoe are characteristic of this Siamese/American Shorthair hybrid.

PROs

- Attractive patterning
- Makes a loyal, affectionate companion
- Gets along well with children and dogs
- Grooming is straightforward
- Individual appearance

CONs

- Unpredictable appearance of kittens
- Not very well known outside North America
- Coloration changes with age
- Must have plenty of attention
- Some Snowshoes can be noisy

BREED PROFILE

Basic type: Shorthaired with a medium-sized body, and a powerful appearance.

Size: Medium.

Colors: Seal point, blue point, chocolate point, lilac point, in two different patterned forms, called mitted and bicolor. In mitted individuals, white areas are restricted to the paws, extending up the back legs, as well as the chin and chest. Bicolors have more white fur, covering between a quarter and half of the coat, with a characteristic white facial blaze between the eyes.

Coat: Short to medium in length, but relatively close-lying and smooth.

Body: Semi-foreign in type, but not resembling the svelte appearance of Siamese, nor the cobby shape of its American Shorthair ancestor.

Tail: Medium in length, tapering slightly along its length.

Head: Broad yet quite short and wedge-shaped, corresponding to an equilateral triangle, with high cheekbones. The ears continue the shape of the skull and are slightly rounded at their tips. Males are likely to develop jowls.

Eyes: Brilliant blue in color, oval in shape and slanting down in the direction of the nose.

Life expectancy: 12-15 years.

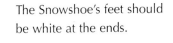

The Snowshoe's feet should be white at the ends.

SHOW STANDARD

The markings are very important, and there must be white on all the paws. The tail should not resemble that of a Siamese, and any deviation in the eye color is penalized. The quality of the coat is important too. Older cats may develop shading on the flanks.

Sphynx

Hairless cats were first recorded from Mexico in the early 1900s, but this strain died out. Today's Sphynx are descended from a single kitten born in Toronto, Canada, in the 1970s, and their numbers have been increased by outcrossings to the Devon Rex in particular. They may not look beautiful, but they are cats with real personality.

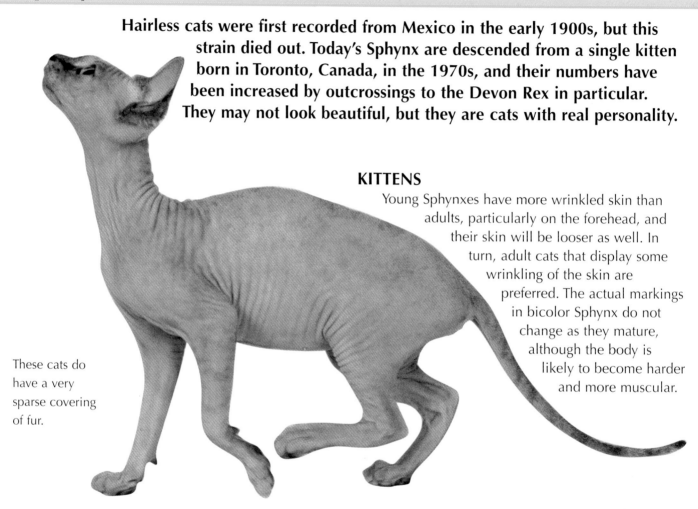

KITTENS
Young Sphynxes have more wrinkled skin than adults, particularly on the forehead, and their skin will be looser as well. In turn, adult cats that display some wrinkling of the skin are preferred. The actual markings in bicolor Sphynx do not change as they mature, although the body is likely to become harder and more muscular.

These cats do have a very sparse covering of fur.

PROs
- Highly affectionate
- Unique patterning
- An ideal indoor companion
- Will not leave large amounts of fur around the home
- Will not suffer hairballs

CONs
- Vulnerable to the cold
- At risk from sunburn
- Excessive wrinkles can lead to localized infection
- Has to be bathed
- Very active

BREED PROFILE

Basic type: Appears hairless, medium in size and with a relatively slender build.

Size: Medium.

Colors: No restrictions, but in this case white areas appear pinkish and black areas will tend to be grayish.

Coat: The skin may appear hairless, but is covered with very fine down, likened to that on the skin of a peach. Longer hair may be present on the extremities of the body, on the ears and tail in particular. Feels warm, owing to the lack of fur, and resembles suede in texture. Whiskers are short and curly.

Body: Medium, with a broad chest and a rounded abdomen.

Tail: Long and narrow, tapering to a tip. The presence of fur at the tip is described as lion-tailed, whereas Sphynxes without hair here are known as rat-tailed.

Head: Wedge-shaped, being slightly longer than wide, with a flat forehead and prominent cheekbones. The muzzle is short and rounded. The ears are very large and broad at the base.

Eyes: Large and lemon-like in shape, slanting down in the direction of the nose.

Life expectancy: 12-15 years.

SHOW STANDARD

There must be no hint of a wavy coat, which highlights the Devon Rex's involvement in the breed's ancestry, or clear evidence of hair on the legs above the ankles. The head must not appear narrow, nor should the body appear weak.

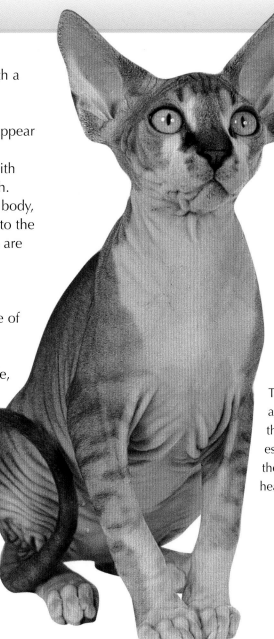

Tabby markings are apparent in this individual, especially on the legs and head.

Tonkinese

The Tonkinese is a controversial breed, having resulted from matings between Burmese and Siamese. This is because, unlike other pure-bred cats, it does not breed true, as both these other breeds can also crop up in Tonkinese litters. This in no way detracts from the Tonkinese's friendly nature though.

The Natural Mink form of the Tonkinese.

KITTENS

Young Tonkinese are always much lighter in color at birth than adults. Their coloration develops slowly and may not be fully developed for two years. All Tonkinese have blue eyes at birth, which will change over several months to that of the color variety concerned.

PROs

- Attractive, easy-care coat
- Very playful and attentive nature
- Excellent companion
- Range of colors to choose from
- Temperature changes unlikely to affect coat color

CONs

- Coat coloration slow to develop
- Hard to assess exhibition potential of young cats
- Very active nature
- Does not breed true
- Males develop a more chunky appearance

BREED PROFILE

Basic type: Shorthaired, smooth-coated with a semi-foreign appearance overall.

Size: Medium.

Colors: Include mink, blue mink, natural mink, platinum mink, honey mink, and champagne, plus tortoiseshell variants. In the UK, however, these colors are named differently, following the usual convention for pointed varieties. The natural mink is known as the brown.

Coat: Relatively short and close-lying, silky and soft in texture with a glossy sheen.

Body: Not as extreme as that of the Siamese but certainly not cobby either. Rectangular, with the back sloping slightly downwards from the rump to the shoulders.

Tail: Can be extended forwards approximately to the shoulder blades, and tapers slightly along its length.

Head: A modified wedge-shape, being slightly longer than wide, with high cheekbones. The ears are positioned on the sides of the head, emphasizing the wedge shape of the face, and are directed slightly forwards, giving an alert appearance.

Eyes: Almond-shaped on the upper side, but more rounded below, well spaced and slanted at an oblique angle upwards towards the ears. Deep coloring preferred.

Life expectancy: 12-15 years.

Blue Mink. The depth of coat coloration may vary slightly between individuals.

SHOW STANDARD

The eyes must not have a true oriental appearance, and yet they should also not be rounded, but intermediate. There should not be any signs of tabby barring, nor must the head have a rounded shape or an obvious nose break.

Tonkinese

Origins

The first example of the Burmese breed seen in the West is now believed to have actually been a Tonkinese, based on breeding records. The only way to guarantee pure Tonkinese offspring in a litter is by mating a Burmese and a Siamese together. This was the approach used by the first breeder in the United States to develop these cats seriously in the 1940s, although he called them Golden Siamese at this stage, because of their distinctive coloration. The name Tonkinese was introduced later, being derived from the Gulf of Tonkin, which separates Burma, home of the Burmese, from Thailand, where the Siamese originated.

Breeding

On average, in every litter of Tonkinese cats, half will be Tonkinese, while a quarter will be Siamese and the other quarter will be Burmese, in terms of coloration. This happens because of the unique way in which the genes for Tonkinese coloring are passed from one generation to the next. Those cats that are produced in Tonkinese litters but are not Tonkinese are described as Tonkinese variants. Their eye coloration offers the simplest way to recognize them while young, because the coat color of these cats is slower to change as they mature. Blue or yellow eyes in the young cats are likely to be suggestive of Tonkinese variants, compared with the blue-green eyes that typify most Tonkinese.

Brown Tortoiseshell, displaying cream and brown coloration.

The Points

Tonkinese do have slightly darker points on the extremities of their bodies, but the contrast is far less marked than in the case of Siamese. In addition, whereas cold weather tends to deepen and emphasize the depth of contrast between the point coloration of the Siamese and its lighter body color, this tends not to apply in the case of Tonkinese cats.

Natural Mink kitten.

123

LONGHAIRED CATS

A Lilac Tortiepoint
Himalayan—a breed that was
created out of interest in the
genetic nature of the
colorpointed characteristic.

The earliest examples of longhaired cats are believed to have originated in Turkey. From here they were then introduced to France, and became highly sought after as pets among the wealthy. Contemporary portrayals of such cats reveal that they were markedly different in appearance from the leading longhaired cats of today.

Their coats were considerably shorter, but down the intervening years breeders have concentrated on developing this feature, especially in the case of the popular Persian breed, which has the longest coat of any cat. Its individual hairs may measure more than five inches long. This change has come about as the result of selective breeding, although it is not just a coincidence that longhaired cats originated in more northerly areas.

The popular Norwegian Forest Cat has a coat that has not become as long as that of the selectively bred Persian, but still affords these outdoor cats very effective protection in their homeland where they have evolved naturally over the course of many centuries. The same applies in the case of the Siberian, a northern Russian breed that is now becoming much better known in the West, and also the very popular Maine Coon, which was the first breed to emerge in North America, being highly valued as a farm cat, used to working outside in all weathers.

The appearance of today's longhaired breeds is still likely to vary quite noticeably through the year, being influenced by the climate. Cats that are thought to be related to the original form of the Persian, such as the Turkish Angora, still reflect the climate of their natural landscape in their molting pattern.

In the winter months, when the weather is often very cold, they have a relatively profuse coat, which helps to protect them in these freezing conditions. Then, in the spring, these cats undergo a heavy molt, losing much of their longer fur, so that they closely resemble shorthairs at this stage. This reflects the fact that, although the winters can be bitter, so the summers are usually very hot, which makes it important for these cats to shed their winter coats beforehand.

This change can still be seen in the Persian today, as well as other breeds, causing a major transformation in their appearance, especially since the characteristic ruff of longer fur around the neck disappears at this stage. Dedicated grooming is particularly necessary at this stage as well, so as to prevent longhaired cats swallowing this molted fur when they groom themselves. Otherwise, it can accumulate, forming a hairball that will create an obstruction in the cat's stomach.

Non-pedigree Longhair

The longhaired characteristic is often seen in the case of non-pedigree cats, but generally, even when adult, their coats are far less profuse than those of pure-bred cats. There may also be occasions when pure-bred longhairs such as Persians mate with such individuals, and then the coats of the resulting kittens are likely to be longer.

KITTENS

The coats of non-pedigree kittens are always shorter than those of adult cats at first, and it will take some months until they acquire their full-length coats, depending to some extent on the time of the year.

PROs

- Highly distinctive cats
- Well protected in cold weather
- Bred in a wide range of colors and patterns
- Friendly and affectionate by nature
- Readily obtainable

CONs

- Pure-colored examples are rare
- Will need regular daily grooming
- Coat can hide ticks very effectively
- Face shape can be variable
- Less pronounced frill than in other longhairs

The patterning of Bicolor Non-pedigree Longhairs can be exceedingly variable.

BREED PROFILE

Basic type: Longhaired or semi-longhaired, with the coat being more profuse in some cases than others, depending on ancestry. Usually quite a stocky build.

Size: Medium, but some of these cats can be large.

Colors: Colors correspond to those seen occurring naturally in European cats, such as brown, black, blue, and red ("ginger"), usually broken by some white, which may just be restricted to the vicinity of the throat. Tabby markings are common, as are tortoiseshell variants.

Coat: Relatively long, thick and soft, but variable in length.

Body: Medium-sized, often powerful, not extreme in type and with reasonably stout legs.

Tail: Medium in length, frequently quite broad at the base and covered with long fur.

Head: Rounded in shape, and often variable in width. The ears are likely to be medium in size, with longer hair known as furnishings usually evident inside. Tend to be rounded in shape, and males may develop evident jowls as they mature, creating the impression of a double chin.

Eyes: Typically quite rounded, although may be almond-shaped, often being located quite centrally on the head.

Life expectancy: 12-15 years.

SHOW STANDARD

These cats are frequently exhibited in classes for non-pedigree or household pets at shows. Their variation in appearance means that there are no prescribed judging standards, but condition is very important, to catch the judge's eye. Longhairs must be immaculately groomed therefore, to show at their best.

Non-pedigree Longhair

Tabby Patterning in Longhairs

The tabby markings in Non-pedigree cats are far less distinctive than in their shorthaired counterparts. This is simply a reflection of differences in the structure of the coat, rather than being a dilution of the patterning itself. In a shorthair, where there is little undercoat, the top coat will be sleek, reinforcing the dark tabby patterning present on the hairs here, which overlay each other. With a denser and unmarked undercoat, however, the top coat cannot lie as flat, and this means that the tabby patterning does not appear to be so strong. This is especially evident in the case of paler tabby variants such as reds, although much depends on the specific length of the cat's coat. Black tabby markings still stand out clearly, in the case of brown tabbies, because there is more contrast between the colors in this case.

Other Coat Differences

The purity of colors often differs between non-pedigree longhairs and their pure-bred relatives. This applies even in the case of cats with black fur, as this often has a brownish hue in the case of non-pedigrees, which would not be permitted in pure-bred individuals.

Bicolors are commonly seen in the case of Non-pedigree Longhairs, but here the patterning is far more random than in the case of pure-bred cats. The amount of white in the coat, for example, can be much greater in Non-pedigrees, where there are no established judging standards. Intermingling of white and colored hairs where these areas come into contact is also quite common in Non-pedigrees but would be outlawed under show standards for pure-bred cats.

RIGHT: This longhaired cat has a relatively profuse coat, being the result of a mating between a Persian and an ordinary Non-pedigree.

LEFT: Tabby patterning is common in Non-pedigree Longhairs, but may not always be very distinctive.

Longhaired American Curl

As with many of the most dramatic changes that can affect a cat's appearance, the American Curl characteristic was first seen in a stray non-pedigree kitten. Discovered in Lakewood, California, back in 1981, this young cat displayed the unusual curled ears that have become the primary feature of the breed today.

Coloration is not considered as being of significance in this breed.

KITTENS

The ears of all the kittens in a litter of America Curls look normal at first, and then signs of curling start to become apparent in some individuals from about four to seven days old. The ears will remain curled for about seven weeks, before finally they start to unfurl. Once a young cat is about six months old, its ear carriage will be established for life.

PROs

- Highly unusual appearance
- Hardy, easy-care cat
- Very friendly and affectionate
- Curling has not created ear problems
- Bred in many colors

CONs

- Open ears may attract unwelcome attention from young children
- Still a scarce breed
- Longhaired form even scarcer than the shorthaired
- Likes to explore outdoors
- Slow to mature

BREED PROFILE

Basic type: Semi-longhaired, with a semi-foreign type. Elegant, with a well proportioned body.

Size: Medium.

Colors: Any colors or patterns are acceptable in this breed, including colorpoints.

Coat: Medium length, with very little undercoat. Has a fine, silky texture. Ear furnishings—hair within the ears themselves—stick out from the folds and are clearly apparent. Desirable lynx-like tufts of hair may also be evident on the tips of the ears.

Body: Intermediate between the classic foreign appearance of the Siamese, and the cobby shape of the American Shorthair. The legs are relatively thick.

Tail: Relatively long, but in proportion to the body.

Head: Wedge-shaped, but with a reasonable length of muzzle, so that it is longer than its width. The ears themselves are relatively large, and rounded at the tips, which should point to the midline of the body.

Eyes: Large, colorful, and walnut-shaped. Colorpoints must have blue eyes.

Life expectancy: 12-15 years.

SHOW STANDARD

Great emphasis is placed on the size and shape of the ears, and other associated features such as the furnishings, and the degree of curl, which has tended to increase through selective breeding.

The length of the coat of the American Curl still rather resembles that of its Non-pedigree ancestor.

Angora

This breed has been described rather confusingly under several names, with its appearance being intended to replicate that of the traditional Angora breed, now better known as the Turkish Angora (see pages 182-5). The Angora is essentially a semi-longhaired form of the Oriental Shorthair, with a similar temperament.

KITTENS

Their coats at birth are shorter than those of adult Angoras, and their eyes are always blue. Litters are traditionally larger than those of the Turkish Angora, often comprising four or five kittens, which is a reflection of their Oriental ancestry.

White Angora, the traditional color associated with the breed.

PROs

- Easy-care coat
- Highly affectionate
- Very playful
- Available in a good choice of colors
- Get along well together

CONs

- Not the traditional Angora
- Needs plenty of attention
- Quite vocal
- Matures at an early age
- Adult males may have jowls

BREED PROFILE
Basic type: Semi-longhair, with a long, lithe body.
Size: Medium.
Colors: Whites have tended to be favored, but a host of other colors have also been created, predominantly but not exclusively self-colors such as lavender and chestnut. Patterned varieties are now being seen more commonly as well.
Coat: Medium-length, fine and silky in texture, lying close against the skin because of a relative lack of undercoat, and generally longer on the underparts.
Body: Long, slender neck with a rather tubular-shaped body. The legs are long and slim, with the hind legs being longer. The paws are small and oval in shape.
Tail: Continues the line of the body, being long, thin, well covered in fur and tapering along its length.

Head: Wedge-shaped head, creating a triangular impression, reinforced by the large, upright ears. The nose is long and straight, without any stop.
Eyes: Well spaced, almond-shaped, usually green in color and sloping towards the nose. Odd-eyed individuals are known, in the case of whites.
Life expectancy: 12-14 years.

SHOW STANDARD
It has proved possible to improve the type of these cats by back-crossing to Oriental Shorthairs. All the kittens born are then shorthaired, but some carry the longhaired gene, and so are valuable to the breeding program, although unfortunately they cannot be distinguished by sight, but only by trial matings.

Red Silver
Shaded, one of
the newer
varieties.

Balinese

These very graceful cats are the longhaired counterpart of the Siamese, corresponding to this breed in all respects other than their coat length. They make superb companions, provided that you have enough time to devote to your pet's needs. The Balinese is a breed that must have plenty of attention.

KITTENS

At birth they lack the distinctive pointed coloration, which starts to appear gradually over the first few weeks of their lives. It can take up to a year for young kittens to develop their full coloration. Their coats are also much shorter than those of adult Balinese at first, but they will soon show signs of becoming fluffy.

Seal Point—the darkest variety.

PROs

- Exceedingly graceful appearance
- Grooming needs are straightforward
- Affectionate and playful
- Gets along well with other cats
- Receptive to training

CONs

- Can be an effective hunter
- Frequently very noisy
- Athletic—may climb up drapes
- Often intolerant of cow's milk
- May suffer from a squint

BREED PROFILE

Basic type: Semi-longhaired, with a very graceful appearance.
Size: Medium.
Colors: Include seal point, blue point, chocolate point, lilac point, cream point, red point, as well as tortie points and lynx (tabby) points in these different colors, including torbie (tortie-lynx) points, although not all have universal recognition.
Coat: Medium-length, with a fine, silky texture. Lies relatively flat, owing to the lack of an undercoat.
Body: Lithe and graceful, with the legs being slim and proportionate, ending in oval paws. The hind legs are slightly longer than the front legs.
Tail: Relatively long and tapering, with a plume-like appearance thanks to the length of the fur here.
Head: Wedge-shaped and long. Relatively large ears, set on the diagonal, which emphasize the triangular shape of the head when viewed from the front.
Eyes: Almond-shaped, sloping down towards the nose and must be a pure, bright shade of blue.
Life expectancy: 12-15 years.

SHOW STANDARD

Tabby markings are often apparent on the points of Cream Point and Red Point Siamese, especially while they are young—hopefully, these should fade with age. Darker shading often develops on the flanks in the case of Seal Point Balinese especially, once they are several years old.

Red Point—one of the newer colors.

Balinese

Origins

Odd longhaired individuals had cropped up in litters of Siamese for many years before the Balinese became recognized as a breed in the 1950s. Indeed, many Siamese breeders were strongly opposed to this move, because they feared that this would increase the number of longhaired kittens turning up unexpectedly in litters of their cats.

The first accounts of longhaired kittens of this type date back to the 1920s, and it is likely that this gene may have originally been introduced as a result of cross-breeding with Turkish Angoras that took place occasionally at that stage. The first determined attempt to develop longhaired Siamese into a breed in their own right was carried out by a breeder in California.

A Chocolate Lynx Point—a tabby variant.

Choosing Names

Opposition from Siamese breeders meant that the description of Longhaired Siamese could not be considered as a name for these cats, so breeders decided to call them Balinese instead. This was chosen not just as a result of its proximity to Thailand, which is the home of the Siamese, but also because the elegance of the native dancers on this Indonesian island reflect the cat's movements.

The Current Situation

Today, with more Balinese varieties having been developed, there is a general tendency for only the four traditional Siamese point colors to be recognized as Balinese. Cream and Red Points, as well as Lynx and Tortie Points are now frequently described as Javanese, mirroring the situation with the Siamese where a division exists between the old and new color varieties.

Playing Games

It is possible to teach a Balinese cat to walk on a harness attached to a leash, so that you can exercise your pet safely outdoors, without any fear of the cat running away. A climbing frame is a good idea if these cats are housed indoors, taking account of their active nature, and you should also offer them a good choice of toys. A Balinese may even learn to be a retriever, bringing a toy ball back to you to throw again, just like a dog!

A Tortie Seal Point. Tortie markings usually stand out clearly in this case.

Birman

The distinctive Birman displays a unique patterning, which helps to set the breed apart from all other colorpointed longhaired cats. It is a very elegant cat that thrives in relatively quiet surroundings, not being as boisterous and assertive by nature as some other breeds of Asiatic origin.

KITTENS

Young Birmans appear white or creamy-white at birth, lacking any trace of their characteristic patterning. Their coat is also like that of a shorthaired cat at this early age, but soon starts to grow. It can take a year for the distinctive pointed coloration to develop fully.

A Seal Point and Blue Point Birman together, showing the difference in coloration.

PROs

- Affectionate and gentle by nature
- Ideal companion for someone living alone
- Coat care not too demanding
- Placid and not disruptive in the home
- Home-loving

CONs

- Can be fussy about their food
- Some individuals can be nervous
- No clear indication of adult show potential evident in kittens
- Do not like lively, noisy surroundings
- Not especially playful

BREED PROFILE

Basic type: Semi-longhaired, long-bodied but rather stocky cat.

Size: Medium.

Colors: Seal point, blue point, chocolate point, lilac point, cream point, red point, as well as tortie points and lynx (tabby) points in these different colors, including torbie (tortie-lynx) points. The most distinctive features, however, are so-called "white gloves" covering the front paws, and more extensive white "gauntlets" extending up the hind legs to just below the hocks.

Coat: Semi-long, with a silky texture and ideally forming a full ruff around the neck, with the fur on the stomach being slightly curled.

Body: Long and strong, with thick-set legs of medium length, ending in large, rounded paws.

Tail: Medium-long, and in proportion to the body, with a bushy appearance.

Head: Broad and rounded, with a flat area in front of the ears, which are well spaced and medium in size. The cheeks are round, and the chin is well developed.

Eyes: Angled slightly towards the nose, with a slightly oval shape instead. They must be a deep shade of blue.

Life expectancy: 12-15 years.

SHOW STANDARD

Deviations to the white patterning on the lower limbs, such as colored toes, are serious faults, as is a marked lack of symmetry. Nor should there be any additional white areas, below the jaws for example.

Young Birman kittens develop their distinctive patterning only as they grow older.

Birman

Origins

The Birman is a breed that has an air of mystery attached to it. Known as the Sacred Cat of Burma, its ancestors were supposedly kept as temple guardians in its homeland. A pair of Birmans were supposedly given to two French adventurers, who helped to repel an attack on a temple. On the long journey back to France, the male died, but by this stage the queen was pregnant, and gave birth shortly after its arrival in France. Various other breeds were then used to maintain the Birman bloodline in the West. Certainly, it is a composite breed today, with Siamese, Colorpoint Longhairs and others having contributed to its early development. It first became recognized for show purposes in France in 1925, and then became popular in Germany. The breed did not reach North America until 1959, however, and was then not seen in Britain for a further five years.

Cream Point—the palest variant.

The Mystery Continues

As far as can be ascertained, no further Birman cats had ever reached the West. This led to a suggestion that the breed was simply created in France. However, just to confound this speculation, an American cat enthusiast managed to gain access to Tibet and returned to the United States in 1960 with a pair of kittens. Christened Tibetan Temple Cats, they subsequently proved to be identical to Birmans in appearance.

How Birmans Gained Their White Paws

Legend tells how a dying monk at a temple devoted to Tsun-Kyan-Kse, who was the goddess of migrating souls, was touched by his favorite cat called Sinh at the moment of his death. His soul then entered the cat's body, with Sinh's fur becoming golden and its orange eyes transformed to sapphire blue, like those of the goddess herself. Only where the cat had been touching the monk with its paws did its fur remain white.

Blue Tabby Point, displaying its individual patterning.

Himalayan

Sometimes known as the Colorpoint Longhair, this breed is also affectionately called the Himmie. Its name Himalayan stems from that given to the gene responsible for its colorpointed appearance. These cats are gentle giants, making great companions for those who have sufficient time to attend to their grooming needs.

KITTENS

The coat of Himalayan kittens is short, but is already fluffy in appearance. White in color at birth, the point color of the young cats will start to emerge in a few days, taking slightly longer to become apparent in pale varieties. Ultimately, the points—comprising the mask, legs, feet, and tail—should display an even depth of coloration.

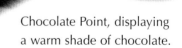

Chocolate Point, displaying a warm shade of chocolate.

PROs

- Appealing, relaxed nature
- Home-loving
- Gets along well with dogs and cats
- Little desire to hunt
- Affectionate companion

CONs

- Coat needs considerable grooming
- Tends to snore
- Relatively large appetite
- Long coat may affect allergy sufferers
- Tear staining can be a problem

BREED PROFILE

Basic type: Longhaired, with a fine texture. Large with a cobby body, and short-legged.

Size: Large.

Colors: Seal point, chocolate point, blue point, lilac point, cream and red points, as well as lynx (tabby) and tortie point variants of these solid point colors, plus torbie points, which display both tortie and lynx point coloring.

Coat: Long and dense, glossy in appearance and with a silky texture. There is a frill present on the chest between the front legs, extending back over the shoulders, while the paws display tufts of fur.

Body: Cobby, with a muscular, deep chest, massive shoulders, a level back, and a large rump. The legs are short and powerful, ending in solid, round paws.

Tail: Short, in proportion to the size of the body, and bushy.

Head: Large and round, with a very broad skull. The cheeks are full, and the nose is short and broad, with the jaws being powerful.

Eyes: Well spaced and round, deep blue in color.

Life expectancy: 12-15 years.

SHOW STANDARD

Tabby patterning is often present in the case of both Cream and Red Points, especially while they are young. On the other hand, darker colors such as Seal Points are likely to develop shading on the sides of their bodies, which darken with age.

Cream Point. The point coloration is less distinctive in this case.

Himalayan

Origins

It was a Swedish geneticist who created this bred simply as an experiment, rather than with the aim of developing a new variety that would appeal to cat fanciers around the world. His intention was to investigate if it was possible to introduce the Himalayan gene, as seen in the Siamese, into the Persian Longhair bloodline, using a White Persian and Siamese cats. A further study into this area of feline genetics followed, being carried out by a doctor from the Harvard Medical School in the United States and a prominent breeder in the early 1930s. It took six years before the first kitten displaying the required characteristics was breed.

This particular research program encouraged other breeders who were intrigued by the prospect of creating what would effectively be a Colorpoint Persian. In Britain, breeders followed the U.S. breeding program to create similar cats, which were ultimately recognized for show purposes before their U.S. counterparts. Having introduced the coloration of the Siamese, breeders then concentrated on refining the type of these cats so that today they are indistinguishable from Persian Longhairs in terms of their type.

Blue Point. The blue contrasts with the glacial white body color.

Himmie Varieties

One of the features of these cats is that the mask tends to cover virtually all the face, being especially pronounced in males. In the case of Lynx Points, the characteristic M-shaped tabby marking will be present on the forehead, but tabby markings may be more conspicuous in some cases than others, with broken rings extending up the legs and evident on the tail. Barring is restricted to the front of the hind leg, with the coloration behind being solid. Tortie Points should display cream or red patches on all their points, although the precise markings are again highly variable between individuals.

Seal Tabby Point, displaying good contrast in its coat.

Maine Coon

This hardy breed has grown greatly in popularity over recent years, so that it has now become the most popular pure-bred cat worldwide, available in a wide range of varieties. The Maine Coon is a lively companion, although it is not a breed that takes well to being closely confined in the home.

Silver Tortie Tabby. This is essentially a female-only variety.

KITTENS

Their coats are quite short at first, with their eyes being blue and opening for the first time when the kittens are about a week old. This color changes gradually over the course of successive weeks. The large adult size of these cats means that they mature slowly.

PROs

- Easy to care for
- Grooming is straightforward
- Energetic and playful
- Makes a good family pet
- Readily available

CONs

- Tends to roam
- Relatively costly to feed
- Can be quite vocal
- Sheds heavily, especially in springtime
- May sleep in odd localities

BREED PROFILE

Basic type: Longhaired, although the coat is of variable length, being shorter over the head and shoulders. Large and muscular in terms of its overall appearance.

Size: Large.

Colors: Solid color grouping features white (in blue-eyed, orange-eyed, odd-eyed, and green-eyed varieties), cream, red, blue, and black. Also mackerel or classic tabby variants, bicolors, smokes and shaded varieties, tortoiseshells of various types, and torbies (tortie tabbies).

Coat: Glossy top coat, which is at its longest over the back and flanks, compared with the rest of the body, although there is a distinct ruff present around the sides of the face, extending down to the chest, which is especially evident in males.

Body: Broad-chested and muscular, with a long back, and powerful but shorter legs, conveying a rectangular impression in profile.

Tail: Long and very well covered with fur.

Head: Medium in length, with the width being slightly less, although mature males do have evident jowls. The muzzle is relatively square, with the nose being slightly concave in profile. The ears are large and tall, well spaced and pointed at their tips.

Eyes: Widely spaced, full and round, tilting slightly obliquely. Typical colors are shades of green, copper or gold, which can be unrelated to that of the coat, with blue confined to white cats.

Life expectancy: 12-15 years.

SHOW STANDARD

The paws must be tufted, and generally, in the case of bicolors or particolors, the total amount of white fur should not exceed a third of the total, with colored areas predominating. Bear in mind that females are significantly smaller than males in this breed.

Tabby and white patterning is always highly individual.

Maine Coon

Origins

This breed arose in Maine, on the eastern seaboard of the United States, probably initially around the ports here. Many ships from Europe and elsewhere were visiting in the late 1700s, and undoubtedly many brought cats with them from Europe. Early settlers coming to America also traveled with cats, some of which probably escaped once they reached land. All these different influences probably helped to shape the breed of today in the early stages of its development.

The Maine Coon acquired its unusual name not just as a reflection of its area of origin, but also because many of these cats were tabbies, and so had a striped tail. This was similar to that of the raccoon, a mammal often seen in this part of North America, to the extent that there were those who believed the Maine Coon was the result of cross-breeding between these cats and 'coons, as they were locally known.

As settlers left Maine and headed west, they took cats with them, and so began the next phase in the Maine Coon's history. The breed soon adapted and evolved into a hardy farm cat, providing not just companionship but also a vital means of controlling rodents that could threaten food production. It was no surprise, therefore, that Maine Coons were exhibited in their own classes at the early agricultural shows, long before there were organized cat shows, confirming their importance alongside that of other farm livestock.

Competition was fierce, but among the early examples of the breed that came to prominence was a black and white individual that went under the name of Captain Jenks of the Horse Marines. It was owned by a Mr. F. Pierce, who was the first to describe the breed back in 1861.

Subsequently, Maine Coons became prominent at the early cat shows, with a representative of the breed winning overall at the major 1895 Madison Square Garden Show event, but then they suffered a dramatic fall in popularity. In spite of their impressive size, which means they rank among the largest of today's natural (as distinct from hybridized) breeds, and an excellent temperament, they became popularly perceived as nothing more than farm cats.

LEFT: Environmental influences have shaped the Maine Coon into the cat seen today.

RIGHT: Red Silver Classic Tabby and White, with the characteristic blotched patterning.

Maine Coon

As America started to develop into a more urbanized society, so city-dwellers focused their interest on exotic breeds brought from Europe, such as the Persian Longhair. This was how things remained for more than seventy years, with the Maine Coon banished to farms, until breeders came to appreciate their heritage, and a reassessment of the breed led to it finally being recognized for show purposes in 1976.

There was also considerable overseas interest in Maine Coons once early examples of the breed were seen in Europe shortly afterwards. In barely twenty years, it has since become the most popular breed in the world, with one leading international pet food manufacturer even producing a special food for these cats.

Red—often displays slight tabby markings. Note the prominent ear tufts and ruff.

Stories Surrounding the Maine Coon

It is sometimes claimed that the Maine Coon is a direct descendent of the Norwegian Forest Cats owned by the French Queen Marie Antoinette, whose cats were sent to America to escape from the turmoil of the French Revolution of 1789, although Marie Antoinette was imprisoned and executed (in October 1793) before she could flee to join her pets. It is

likely that these cats would have generated greater attention if this were true.

Others stories suggest that cats that contributed to the ancestry of the breed were brought over regularly from Europe by a Captain Coon, helping to explain their name. Once again, however, there is no real evidence for this, any more than there is to support the suggestion that a group of Turkish Angoras obtained in their homeland bred with local cats in Maine, and so serve to explain the breed's origins.

Maine Coons are cats that thrive if allowed outdoors.

Maine Coon

A Working Cat

The Maine Coon evolved on similar lines to the Norwegian Forest Cat because both were working breeds. Although longhaired, the Maine Coon's coat needs relatively little grooming. Its top coat is water-resistant, so that even in heavy rain the cat's dense undercoat is protected from water and helps to keep it warm. Its large size also helps the Maine Coon to maintain its body temperature more easily, effectively increasing its mass relative to its surface area. In the spring, these cats lose most of their thick coat, mirroring the seasonal change taking place, to the extent that their appearance will become radically

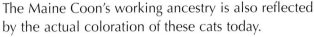

transformed at this stage. The most obvious sign is that the characteristic ruff disappears, with the coat becoming far less profuse overall, until the following fall when it regrows again, prior to winter.

The Maine Coon's working ancestry is also reflected by the actual coloration of these cats today.

Individuals with tabby markings are still very common, as are bicolors, rather than highly refined self-colors. The small tufts of hair on the tips of the ears, which are evident in many examples of the breed, further emphasize its natural, unrefined appearance.

Signs of a Seaborne Existence Today?

An unusual behavior often displayed by Maine Coons is the way in which they will often seek out confined spaces to sleep, sometimes even venturing into open cupboards for this purpose, and often choosing to lie at unusual angles too. It has been suggested that this is a reflection of the way in which their ancestors might have slept on boats, curling up out of the way wherever there was a quiet space available to them. This seems unlikely, however, bearing in mind that much of the breed's development occurred on land, particularly as cats in general will sleep in snug retreats wherever they feel secure.

The variation in appearance that can occur is evident by contrasting the appearance of this Silver Tortie Tabby with the one shown on page 146.

Norwegian Forest Cat

A breed that has been shaped very little by selective breeding, the Norwegian Forest Cat has remained essentially unaltered in appearance down the centuries. It has now become increasingly popular as a pet, thriving particularly where it has space to roam.

Cream—a relatively unusual variety of this cat.

KITTENS

They are shorthaired at birth, and have blue eyes at first. The coat is soft and fluffy at this stage, with the coarser guard hairs emerging subsequently, as the cats grow older. Norwegian Forest Cats develop slowly and are unlikely to be fully mature until they are at least three years old.

PROs

- Hardy, generally healthy cats
- Attractive, wild appearance
- Quite quiet
- An ideal family pet
- Lively and inquisitive

CONs

- Likes to explore outdoors
- Slow to develop
- Agile, enthusiastic climbers
- Toms are very territorial
- Very energetic

BREED PROFILE

Basic type: Semi-longhaired and large. A powerfully built, relatively tall cat.

Size: Large.

Colors: All European colors are allowed, with associated tabby and tortie patterning, as well as shaded, smokes, and bicolors. The black and white bicolor is the traditional variety. Colorpointed patterning and Oriental colors such as chocolate and lilac are not acceptable.

Coat: Smooth, water-repellent top coat with a thick, dense undercoat beneath. In the winter, these cats display a full ruff, extending from the shoulders down over the chest, and also so-called long "knickerbockers" on the hind legs.

Body: Large, with a powerful bone structure. A long body, with correspondingly long legs and powerful paws.

Tail: Long, extending round to reach the neck, and bushy in appearance.

Head: Has a very distinctive equilateral triangular shape when seen from the front, with the outer edges of the ears continuing the lines of the face. They have furnishings of hair here and should have tufts of longer hair on the tips as well.

Eyes: Large, set slightly obliquely.

Life expectancy: 12-15 years.

SHOW STANDARD

The front paws naturally turn out slightly, and this is acceptable. The shape of the head is very important, with the gently rounded muzzle enabling this breed to be separated from the square profile seen in the Maine Coon, which it resembles. Any stop in the nose is a fault.

Black Silver and White. Bicolors are common in this breed.

Norwegian Forest Cat

Origins

The Norwegian Forest Cat has evolved on natural lines over the course of centuries in its native Scandinavian homeland. Its origins have been lost in the mists of time, but it has been suggested that the breed might be related to the Turkish Angora. It may well have been the Vikings who took the ancestors of today's Norwegian Forest Cats back to Norway with them, over a thousand years ago. These cats then developed in this colder, wetter landscape, acquiring their waterproof top coat and a dense insulating undercoat to keep them warm.

International Interest

It was only by the 1930s that the breed attracted the interest of cat enthusiasts in its homeland, and then it finally achieved international recognition through FiFe in 1977. It soon became better known in other parts of Europe as a result, and was introduced to the United States, where it has become increasingly popular over recent years. It is very similar to the native Maine Coon breed, but the likelihood is that these cats have simply developed in similar landscapes, and so have evolved to become similar in appearance, and are not directly related.

Black Silver Tortie Tabby and White. The patterning is highly individual.

Fairy Tales

Records suggest that Norwegian Forest Cats were probably most common in the south of the country, close to the border with Sweden. They would roam through the woods, but were also valued around farmsteads, as a means of controlling vermin. The breed is known in its homeland as the Norsk Skogkatt, and frequently features in native folk-tales, having been established in the country for so long. The goddess Freya's wagon was reputedly pulled by two of these cats, and their reputed magical powers have led to them being described as Fairy Cats.

Glycogen Storage Disease

Pure-bred cats are thankfully largely free of inherited problems, but this metabolic illness has been identified in some Norwegian Forest bloodlines in the United States. It is therefore advisable to acquire kittens only from breeding stock that has been screened accordingly.

Black Silver Tortie Tabby and White, displaying composite patterns.

Persian

Odd-eyed White.

This breed now exists in a multitude of colors and varieties. Persians are docile cats by nature, but before acquiring a kitten it is very important to be sure that you are prepared to undertake the grooming that will be required on a daily basis throughout your cat's life, so as to prevent the long coat from becoming matted.

KITTENS

The coat is short in all cases, and there are often specific differences, depending on the variety. Faint tabby markings, known as ghost markings, are not uncommon in Self Persian kittens particularly, but these normally disappear with age, although not always in the case of Self Cream or Red individuals. Chocolate kittens may have slight grayness of the coat at first, while young Smokes lack any hint of their silver undercoat at birth.

PROs

- Magnificent flowing coat
- Home-loving nature
- Disinclined to hunt
- Affectionate by nature
- Quiet and placid

CONs

- Molts heavily, especially in spring
- Regular daily grooming essential
- Prone to hairballs
- Susceptible to tear-staining
- Sometimes snuffles or snores

BREED PROFILE

Basic type: Longhaired, with a fine texture. Large with a cobby body, and short-legged.

Size: Large.

Colors: Include "self" varieties—black, white (blue-eyed, orange-eyed, and odd-eyed variants), cream, red, chocolate, lilac, plus smoke and tipped in these colors, chinchilla, cameo, pewter, golden, shaded silver, tabby, torties, bicolors, and van patterned forms.

Coat: Long and dense, glossy in appearance, and with a silky texture. There is a frill present on the chest between the front legs, extending back over the shoulders, while the paws display tufts of fur.

Body: Cobby, with a powerful, deep chest, massive shoulders, a level back and a large rump. The legs are short and strong, ending in solid, round paws.

Tail: Short, in proportion to the size of the body, and bushy.

Head: Large and round, with a very broad skull. The cheeks are full, and the nose is short and broad, with the jaws being powerful. Ears are small, set low on the head and widely spaced, with round tips.

Eyes: Well spaced and round, deep blue in color.

Life expectancy: 12-15 years.

SHOW STANDARD

The quality of the distinctive coat is very important—this must not have a woolly texture. Color requirements for the different varieties are quite specific, although the presence of white lockets in the case of "self" varieties for example will be penalized.

Lilac and White—a relatively new addition to the Bicolor group.

Persian

Origins

It is thought that the Persian owes its ancestry to the Turkish Angora, but its precise origins are unknown. Certainly, it appears that there was a definite difference between these two breeds by the 1800s, with Persians already being much larger and more impressive cats by this stage.

By the time that cat showing started in Britain in the late 1800s, the Persian was prominent among the early registrations, with the Black Persian being the first breed to be accorded a breed standard for judging purposes. All the different forms of the Persian—of which there are now in excess of sixty—have since been given individual breed status as a result, rather than being recognized simply as distinctive varieties, as applies elsewhere in the world.

Contemporary photographs reveal distinctive differences in type, however, between Persians then and those of today. Their coats overall were far less profuse at that stage, and their heads were smaller and less compact, displaying a much longer muzzle, making them more akin to Non-pedigree Longhairs. These cats may well have played a significant part in the Persian's development at this stage, by helping to introduce new colors to the breed, which is a process that its still continuing today. Most recently, Oriental colors such as chocolate have been transferred to Persian bloodlines.

The Persian now has the longest coat of all domestic cats, as the result of selective breeding over the past century. Not all these changes have necessarily been beneficial, however, with the most extreme form being the so-called Peke-face, with its large head and a dramatically compressed face. This feature often affects the tear drainage from the eyes of ordinary Persians too.

Blue-cream Persian, showing the distinctive ruff of longer fur that is most apparent during the colder, winter months.

Classic Brown Tabby, displaying its black tabby markings.

Black—an even, solid coloration is essential.

Persian

Just inside the lower eyelid, there is a small opening, connecting to the naso-lacrimal dust, which, as its name suggests, carries tear fluid from the eyes. The compact facial shape may cause distortion of this link, and as a result tear fluid overflows out of the eyes and runs down the fur on each side of the nose, causing dark staining. This will need to be wiped away gently with damp cottonwool. The deposits are worse in cold weather. In some cases, surgery may help to improve this condition.

The large size of the head also means that Persians may sometimes be at greater risk of suffering from birthing difficulties, if the head of a kitten becomes trapped in the female's birth canal. In this case, a Caesarean section is likely to be required, to safeguard the kittens and their mother.

Tabby Persians

The long coat of the Persian ensures that the tabby markings are far less distinctive than they are in most other breeds, since the coat is not sleek. The majority of Persians tend to display classic tabby markings. It has been possible to combine tabby patterning with tortoiseshell patterning too, giving rise to what are tortie tabbies, which are also described as patched tabbies. In common with other similar cats, the markings in this case are highly individual.

A Blue Persian has a grayish tone to its coat.

Bicolors

The breeding of bicolor Persians dates back to the early days of the Cat Fancy, when the black and white cats of this type were called magpies. Dark-coated variants still tend to be preferred, simply because the contrast in their coats is most apparent. It proved impossible to stabilize white areas, so now the standard simply requires between a third and a half of the coat of a Persian Bicolor must be white, with both colored and white areas of fur being evident on the face. A white blaze, extending down between the eyes, is often favored. White hairs must not be mixed with colored hairs anywhere on the body though—there should be sharp delineation between these areas of the coat.

Red and White Bicolors, displaying a variation in their depth of coloration.

Persian

Van Patterning

A fairly recent development has been the attempt to establish Van patterns in the case of the Persian. These are based on the traditional appearance of the Turkish Van breed (see page 186-187). Van Persians are therefore predominantly white in color, with the colored areas on their bodies restricted to the head and ears, and the tail. In addition, there can also be up to three small colored spots on the body. There are both bicolor and tricolor forms of Van patterning, with the latter being tortie variants.

Tipped, Smoked, and Shaded

The long fur of the Persian means that varieties that display different coloration along individual hairs can be very impressive, literally sparkling in some cases as they move. The extent to which the dark pigment extends down the individual hairs will have a marked impact on the cat's appearance. The palest variety is the tipped, with the coloration confined literally to the tips of the individual hairs in such cases. This underlies the appearance of the Chinchilla variety, which looks silvery with a hint of black tipping on the coat, or the Shell Cameo.

The shaded varieties, such as the Shaded Silver, are intermediate, being the darker form of the Chinchilla in this case, displaying more extensive pigmentation at the ends of the guard hairs, although the undercoat is pale. In the case of Smoke Persians, however, the dark pigmentation extends almost to the base of the guard hairs. These cats appear dark

A Blue Smoke—the smoke effect is greatest when the cat is moving.

in color, and the contrast with the light undercoat is most apparent when the cat walks, as the long fur momentarily parts over its body, revealing the undercoat. The early examples of the Smoke date back to the 1860s, with the effect being particularly marked in the case of the Black Smoke, thanks to the extreme contrast in the coat. This feature is not just associated with "self" colors, however, and can be seen in tortie variants as well.

A Tortoiseshell Persian. The patterning is entirely random.

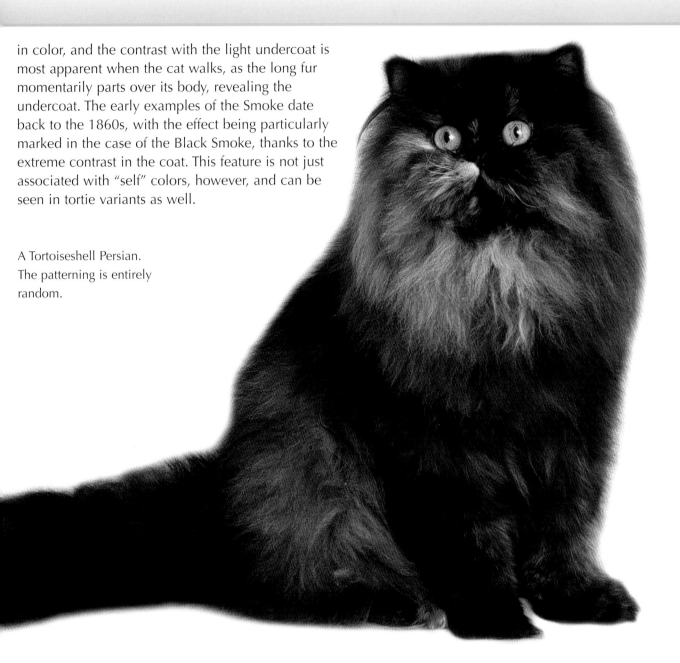

Persian

White Persians

It is actually impossible to distinguish between the three different types of White Persians, because all such kittens have blue eyes at first. Unfortunately, those that subsequently retain this feature throughout their lives are likely to be severely handicapped, as the result of being deaf. Odd-eyed white individuals have restricted hearing, confined to the side of the face corresponding to their orange eye. Deaf cats are at a major disadvantage if they are allowed to wander, simply because they can easily be run over by a vehicle traveling at speed. They will not be alerted by the noise of its imminent approach, and can easily find themselves trapped in the road as a consequence.

Tortie Cameo. These Persians are characterized by red tipping on their white hairs. Colorpoints like this Lynx-pointed variant are being developed.

Peculiarities of the Persian

Studies undertaken by a pet food manufacturer have revealed that, thanks to their flattened facial shape, Persian cats feed in a different way to other breeds. This is why they seem to eat at a slower rate, and it means that they can be at a disadvantage if they are fed together with other cats.

The Persian actually uses the underside of its tongue to scoop up a piece of dry food, flicking this into its mouth. In over half of instances, however, the food falls off the tongue before it can be swallowed, slowing down the Persian's rate of food consumption.

The shape of the Persian's face also means that it is less likely to chew its food, and is more likely to suffer from a build-up of tartar on its teeth. This if left can ultimately lead to loss of teeth. Owning a Persian is therefore not just about grooming, but also keeping its teeth clean. A specially designed food is now available for this breed, with the pieces being almond-shaped, making them easier for the cat to ingest.

Chinchilla kittens. The contrast in their coat is not fully developed at this age.

Pixiebob

Although appearing like a smaller version of the American Bobcat, thanks partly to the shape of its tail, the Pixiebob is a domestic breed that has been developed from a naturally occurring mutation, rather than by hybridization. In fact, it is very unlikely that a Bobcat could be crossed successfully with a domestic cat. Although still quite rare, Pixiebobs make lively companions.

KITTENS

They look rather like miniature adults, although it can be difficult to separate longhaired examples of the breed from shorthaired at this age, as both can occur in the same litter. They display the spotted patterning and ticking on their coats at this early age.

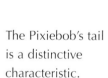

The Pixiebob's tail is a distinctive characteristic.

PROs

- Unique patterning
- Friendly and playful
- Hardy nature
- A cat with great character
- Easy to groom

CONs

- Appearance alters with the season
- Limited availability
- Anatomical shortcomings
- Tail shape and size differ
- Eyes often kept partially closed

BREED PROFILE

Basic type: Medium-longhaired, with a relatively powerful build, and rather variable in size, still being effectively standardized.

Size: Medium to large.

Colors: Only occurs in a brown spotted tabby form.

Coat: Composed of medium length fur typically less than two inches in length, and lies sleek, displaying less of an undercoat than the shorthaired form of the breed, which has rather a stand-off coat.

Body: Long-bodied, with males being larger in size than females. Both display a muscular chest and a deep flank. The legs are relatively long and muscular, with the feet being large.

Tail: Should measure at least two inches, and can extend down to the hocks. Ideally natural, but kinking or curling is acceptable. Carried low, being raised when the cat is alert.

Head: Likened to the shape of a medium or large pear, having a slightly convex (rounded) appearance.

Eyes: Deep set and medium-sized. Can be gold to brown in color, but gooseberry-green acceptable.

Life expectancy: 12-14 years.

SHOW STANDARD

Extra toes, normally prohibited, are considered acceptable in this breed, and up to seven can be present on each foot, all of which must be directed forwards. A wide, slightly convex nose and a broad muzzle are vital features.

The Pixiebob is a distinctive breed currently growing in popularity in North America.

Ragdoll

Generally considered to be the most docile of all breeds, the Ragdoll makes a superb companion, being especially tolerant of and trustworthy with children. Some supervision is still recommended though, if only to ensure that the Ragdoll itself is not hurt by rough handling.

Seal Bicolor, showing the distinctive markings of this variety.

KITTENS
Ragdolls are white at birth, and will start to display initial signs of their coloration only when they are about a week old. Their coats are also short at this early stage in life. They then mature slowly, with this process usually taking three to four years.

PROs

- Exceedingly relaxed temperament
- Friendly with people
- Little interest in hunting
- Straightforward grooming needs
- Disinclined to scratch

CONs

Coloration changes with age
Large size
Has a fatty pad on the underside of the stomach
Likely to be bullied by other cats
Trusting nature may encourage theft

BREED PROFILE

Basic type: Medium-length coat, and a large, powerful body are characteristic of this breed.

Size: Large.

Colors: Seal point, blue point, chocolate point, and lilac point, with three distinctive patterns being recognized, known as colorpoint, mitted, and bicolor.

Coat: Silky and dense, being shortest on the face and on the shoulders, and longest around the neck, becoming longer overall in the winter. The coat is medium-length elsewhere on the body.

Body: Strong, powerful neck and a long, muscular body with a broad chest. The hind legs are slightly longer than the front legs, which are of medium thickness. They end in large, round paws that should display tufts of fur on them.

Tail: Long and tapering slightly along its length.

Head: Relatively large, with well developed cheeks and a rounded muzzle. The ears are broad at the base and tilt forwards slightly, being rounded at the tips, with furnishings of long fur evident in the ears.

Eyes: Oval and large, should be a deep blue in color.

Life expectancy: 12-15 years.

SHOW STANDARD

Makes allowance for the slow maturity of these cats, in terms of their coloration. Poor contrast between the points and body color is considered to be a fault. Any tendency to squint is a very serious flaw.

Blue Mitted, reminiscent of the Ragdoll's Birman ancestor.

Ragdoll

Origins

The Ragdoll's development came about by chance, with the breed arising from a mating in 1965 between a Birman tom and what may have been a White Persian queen, or a similarly colored Non-pedigree Longhair. The breed was first taken to Britain in 1981, and today the Ragdoll enjoys a strong following, among pet seekers as well as exhibitors.

Why Ragdoll?

The name Ragdoll was chosen for these cats because of the way in which they will relax when being picked up, like a ragdoll toy. A myth grew up that guaranteed considerable publicity for the new breed, based on the tale that the queen was run over by a vehicle while pregnant, but she survived. The breeder then put forward the idea that these cats were largely immune to pain as a result, although they possess a perfectly normal pain threshold, as has since been shown.

Blue Mitted kitten. The Ragdoll's patterning is slow to develop fully.

Distinctive Patterning

The appearance of the Colorpoint variety resembles that of the Himalayan, having a well defined and extensive mask, which covers much of the face, with corresponding coloration present on the ears, lower legs, feet, and tail. In contrast, the Mitted form reflects the Birman input into the breed's ancestry, with white mittens present on the front paws, and so-called white boots extending to the hocks (joints on lower legs) on the hind legs. In these cases, darker shading is very likely to develop on the flanks of the body with age.

The appearance of the Bicolor variety is quite different, with dark areas on the head, back, and tail. There is an inverted, symmetrical white V-shaped marking on the nose, which may occasionally be a feature associated with the Mitted form as well. The entire underparts in the Bicolor are white, with the white on the hind legs extending up as far as the hocks themselves. Clear delineation between the colored and white areas is important in this case too. Some small, discrete white patches are, however, permitted in the colored part of the coat.

All three Ragdoll variants are shown here—Mitted, Bicolor, and Pointed.

Longhaired Scottish Fold

Longhaired Scottish Folds are closely related to the shorthaired form of the breed (see pages 108-109), with both often likely to crop up together in litters bred from a shorthaired parent, since they can carry the longhaired gene. Their cuddly appearance is no illusion, as Scottish Folds will prove to be just as friendly as they look.

KITTENS

All the kittens in a litter of a Scottish Fold bred with a Non-Fold (the required pairing to avoid skeletal problems) have normal ears at first. It then takes two to three weeks before the appearance of Scottish Fold kittens begins to alter.

PROs

- Highly affectionate
- Makes a good family pet
- Tolerant by nature
- Gets along well with other cats
- Hardy disposition

CONs

- Scottish Folds must not be mated together
- Both Folds and Non-Folds look similar at birth
- Can suffer skeletal problems
- Requires more grooming than the Shorthair
- Coat length varies through the year

BREED PROFILE

Basic type: Semi-longhaired, with a compact, well rounded body shape.

Size: Medium.

Colors: All colors and varieties are acceptable, although bicolors tend to predominate.

Coat: Semi-long, with a ruff around the neck and britches, which are especially evident in the winter. There should be furnishings in the ears, and toe tufts too. The coat is soft in texture, but double-layered and so stands away from the body.

Body: Rounded and thick-set, with the legs in proportion to the body.

Tail: Must be flexible. Medium-length and tapering to a point, appearing bushy.

Head: Rounded, with a broad, short nose and relatively wide muzzle. Mature tom cats have prominent jowls. The ears are set rather in the position of a cap, not high on the head. They must fold forwards and downwards, ideally being both relatively small and tightly folded, with rounded tips.

Eyes: Large and round, matching the color of the coat.

Life expectancy: 12-15 years.

SHOW STANDARD

The tail must be flexible, and these cats must also be able to walk without any evident signs of difficulty, a problem likely to be linked with Fold-to-Fold pairings, irrespective of their coat length. Non-Folds in litters are therefore very important for breeding purposes, because of their type, differing only in the shape of their ears.

Blue-cream and White. Otherwise known as the Dilute Calico and White, this is a tortoiseshell variety.

Siberian

This ancient northern breed has become much better known in the West over the past twenty years or so. It was originally called the Siberian Forest Cat, but it is probably not closely related to the Norwegian breed known under a similar name. They do have features in common, however, such as their weather-resistant coats.

Varied patterning is a feature of this breed.

KITTENS

The Siberian is a breed that matures slowly, and it can take up to five years for these cats to be fully developed. The distinctive undercoat is a feature that will be seen only in mature individuals. Kittens have shorter coats than those of adult cats.

PROs

- Natural, wild-type appearance
- An entirely domestic breed
- Friendly and lively
- Quiet by nature
- Wide choice of colors and varieties

CONs

- Still quite scarce and therefore likely to be expensive
- Slow to mature
- Likes to explore outdoors
- Not especially keen on being cuddled
- Keen climbers

BREED PROFILE

Basic type: Semi-longhaired to longhaired. Medium in size and quite powerfully built.

Size: Medium-bodied.

Colors: One of the best-known color varieties is the Golden Tabby, with the black tabby patterning offset against the golden agouti coloration of the remainder of the coat. There are few restrictions in terms of exhibiting the Siberian, although white individuals are scarce, and not every organization recognizes the colorpoint variety, sometimes called the Neva Masquerade. The coat texture is variable.

Coat: Double-layered, with the water-repellent glossy top coat offset against the thick undercoat. There is usually a ruff of longer fur on the chest.

Body: Well muscled and medium in size, being greater in length than height. The legs are in proportion to the body, in terms of their length, although the hind legs are longer overall. The feet are rounded in shape and large.

Tail: Medium length, shorter than the body, and tapering to a blunt tip.

Head: Relatively broad, with a rounded muzzle. The ears are also rounded and tilt slightly forwards.

Eyes: Large, well spaced, virtually round. There is no link between coat and eye coloration.

Life expectancy: 12-15 years.

SHOW STANDARD

Allowance is given for the fact that female cats are much smaller than males, and also for the immature appearance of young individuals. Relatively little emphasis is placed on coloration and patterning, compared with other features, notably the cat's overall type (appearance).

The coat is likely to appear shorter in the summer.

Somali

The Somali is the longer-coated form of the Abyssinian (see pages 36-37), and is available in a corresponding range of colors, although it still tends to be less commonly seen. Aside from the length of its coat, it is very similar in temperament, proving to be a personable companion.

Ruddy Somali, better known in the UK as the Usual, corresponding to the original Abyssinian color.

KITTENS

The coat is short at first, before becoming fluffy. It is then likely to take at least a month to start to attain its desired silky appearance. Young Somali kittens are relatively dark at birth, and their lighter ticking and banding may take up to eighteen months to develop to their full extent.

PROs

- Elegant appearance
- Gets along well with dogs and other cats
- Has an extroverted but not dominant nature
- Coat care reasonably straightforward
- Affectionate and friendly

CONs

- Often climbs readily
- These cats can prove to be agile hunters
- Litter sizes relatively small
- Potentially vulnerable to feline leukemia
- Quite vocal, although not very noisy

BREED PROFILE

Basic type: Semi-longhaired with an intermediate type.

Size: Medium.

Colors: Include ruddy (also known as the "usual"), sorrel, blue, chocolate, lavender, cream, red, fawn, black silver, blue silver and sorrel silver, usual tortie, sorrel tortie, blue tortie, chocolate tortie, lilac tortie, and fawn tortie, although not all varieties may be universally recognized.

Coat: Very soft and fine, being of medium-length overall and somewhat shorter over the shoulders. A ruff is preferable, but this may be influenced by the season. Three bands of ticking should be evident on the coat.

Body: Medium-length with a type that lies between the extreme Oriental profile and cobby appearance of the American Shorthair. Legs are in proportion as well, with the oval feet displaying longer tufts of fur.

Tail: Tapers slightly, and displays a full brush of long hair.

Head: Moderate wedge-shape, broad and with a slight nose break. The ears are widely spaced and quite large. Their bright coloration is highlighted by the dark lids.

Eyes: Almond-shaped, slanting down towards the nose.

Life expectancy: 12-15 years.

SHOW STANDARD

The ticking on the coat is not so apparent in the Somali compared with its sleek-haired Abyssinian relative, because of the difference in coat texture. These cats must never have a grayish hue to their coats.

Sorrel Somali, distinguishable by its reddish coloration.

Somali

Origins

The first Somalis appeared unexpectedly in litters of Abyssinians, with the longhaired gene possibly having been introduced from Turkish Angora crosses. Although these kittens cropped up in a number of different countries, including Canada, Australia, and New Zealand, careful study of the bloodlines involved traced them back to British Abyssinian stock, which suggested that the longhaired genes had probably been introduced at some stage during this breed's early development.

These longhaired individuals were frowned upon at this stage, however, and discarded quietly from breeding programs, ending up as pets. But attitudes changed gradually as breeders came to see the appeal of these cats, and so began a move to develop them into a distinctive breed in their own right. The name "Somali" was chosen, simply because of the proximity of this country to Abyssinia (now Ethiopia), where the Abyssinian originated.

The new breed was first exhibited in Australia in 1965, but gaining acceptability in the United States was a longer process, not being achieved until 1979. In the UK, it took an exhibitor to show a litter of Somali kittens at a major show in 1971 for serious discussion about the possibility of developing these cats to start. Even so, it was to be a further twenty years before the breed finally achieved championship status from the major British registration body, the GCCF.

Chocolate Silver. The undercoat of these Somalis affects their appearance.

Appearance

Just as in the case of the Abyssinian, it has proved to be very difficult to breed Somalis without a trace of white fur on the chin, which may also be apparent around the nose. They are ticked tabbies, but in this case, the barring on the legs has been removed by selective breeding. In the case of the silver varieties, the ground color is pure white, enabling these Somalis to be distinguished from those with a golden undercoat that characterizes the equivalent normal variety.

Black Silver. Displays good contrast in its coat.

Turkish Angora

These very elegant cats can resemble shorthairs in the summer, with only the plume of long fur on the tail often revealing their true coat type at this stage. They should not be confused with the Angora (see pages 132-133), being descended from a separate bloodline.

KITTENS

Their coats are short at first, although they do possess the distinctive silky texture at this stage. As the young cats grow older, so the longer coat develops, but this will be partly influenced by the time of year, as this feature is naturally more evident through the winter months.

Black—can develop a brownish hue outdoors in strong sunlight.

PROs

- Elegant, fine-boned appearance
- Coat care is straightforward
- Responsive, lively nature
- Forms a close bond with people
- Get along well with each other

CONs

- Will climb readily
- Likes to wander outdoors
- Can be an adept hunter
- Deafness in those with blue eyes
- Black coats may develop a brownish tinge

BREED PROFILE

Basic type: Semi-longhaired, with a long body and a light build, appearing relatively tall.

Size: Medium.

Colors: Traditionally white, as blue-eyed, orange-eyed or the favored odd-eyed variety, but now bred in a wider range of colors, including black, cream, and red. Bicolors, tabbies, tortoiseshells, and smokes all exist as well.

Coat: Fine and silky in texture, being medium in length on the body, but longer around the chest, creating a ruff here, and the tail also is well plumed.

Body: Long, and lithe, yet muscular. The legs are long, especially the hind legs, so the body slopes up to the tail. The paws are small and round, with the toes being separated by tufts of longer hair.

Tail: Broad at the base, tapering slightly along its length.

Head: Relatively small and wedge-shaped, with the ears being long and pointed and set high on the head, with evident furnishings of long hair inside them.

Eyes: Almond-shaped, with their coloration varying depending on the variety. Silver tabbies should have green or hazel eyes, while other varieties apart from the white all have amber eyes.

Life expectancy: 12-15 years.

White—the traditional color associated with this breed.

SHOW STANDARD

Quality of the coat is very important. This must not be coarse. Color range does not extend to non-traditional colors such as Chocolate or Himalayan patterning.

Turkish Angora

Origins
The Turkish Angora is believed to be one of the oldest breeds of cat in the world, having been first recorded in its Turkish homeland over 500 years ago. It is thought that Italian merchants visiting the region may have taken these cats back with them to Europe, where they became popular in the royal courts. Later, Turkish Angoras were probably crossed with other cats, perhaps helping in the early development of the Persian breed, and started to lose their own popularity.

Red and White Bicolors are becoming more common.

In Danger of Dying Out

The breed takes its name from that formerly given to Turkey's capital city, which is now called Ankara. It was here during the 1960s at the local zoo that a breeding program was started to safeguard the future of what had become a very rare breed by this stage, reduced to a very small number of individuals. Some examples of the breed found their way to Europe and the United States as well, allowing these cats to become reestablished gradually again outside their homeland.

Meanwhile, some breeders tried to recreate the traditional type of the Turkish Angora by using Oriental Shorthairs, which has subsequently led to some confusion. Today, the description of Turkish Angora is used to indicate cats of Turkish descent, with Angora being used for those of Oriental origins. There is still a distinction between these breeds in terms of their appearance, in that the Turkish Angora has small ears, and a shorter, straighter head profile as well.

Why White?

Considerable emphasis is placed on cats displaying pure white coloration in the case of the Turkish Angora breed. It is the odd-eyed form, known in its homeland as *Ankara kedi*, that is regarded as the traditional variety. These white cats have a particularly special significance in Turkey, because of the long-standing belief that the country's former ruler, Ataturk, would be reincarnated in the guise of a white cat of this breed.

A dilute form of the Tortoiseshell, also known as the Blue-cream.

Turkish Van

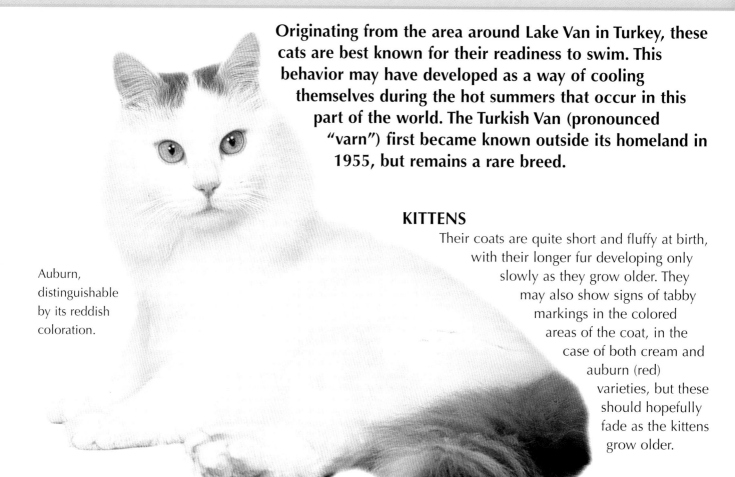

Originating from the area around Lake Van in Turkey, these cats are best known for their readiness to swim. This behavior may have developed as a way of cooling themselves during the hot summers that occur in this part of the world. The Turkish Van (pronounced "varn") first became known outside its homeland in 1955, but remains a rare breed.

Auburn, distinguishable by its reddish coloration.

KITTENS

Their coats are quite short and fluffy at birth, with their longer fur developing only slowly as they grow older. They may also show signs of tabby markings in the colored areas of the coat, in the case of both cream and auburn (red) varieties, but these should hopefully fade as the kittens grow older.

PROs

- Affectionate and friendly
- Adaptable by nature
- A historic breed
- Unusual background
- Coat care straightforward

CONs

- May plunge into the bath
- Quite determined by nature
- Fish in garden ponds may not be safe
- Relatively restricted availability
- Needs very precise markings for show purposes

BREED PROFILE

Basic type: Semi-longhaired with a long, muscular body.

Size: Medium.

Colors: Predominantly creamy-white in color, with the traditional varieties being auburn and cream, in both blue-eyed and odd-eyed combinations, although there are other colors, not all recognized for show purposes, including tortoiseshell and dilute tortoiseshell. Patterning is very important, with a white blaze dividing the colored areas on the head, and the tail also being colored. There may be slight patches of color around the base of the tail as well.

Coat: Long and soft, with a silky texture, being significantly shorter and lighter during the summer months.

Body: Sturdy body, especially in males, with medium-length legs and well rounded toes, with fur between them.

Tail: Medium in length, and well furred.

Head: Short and wedge-shaped, with a long, straight nose and a short muzzle. The ears are large, and are well furnished with hair, being set high up on the head.

Eyes: Large, oval, often amber but with the coloration depending on the variety concerned.

Life expectancy: 12-16 years.

SHOW STANDARD

There may sometimes be small, so-called "thumbprints" of color elsewhere on the cat's body, rather than the head or tail. These are not favored. Also, rings of tabby coloration may be evident on the tail, even in adults.

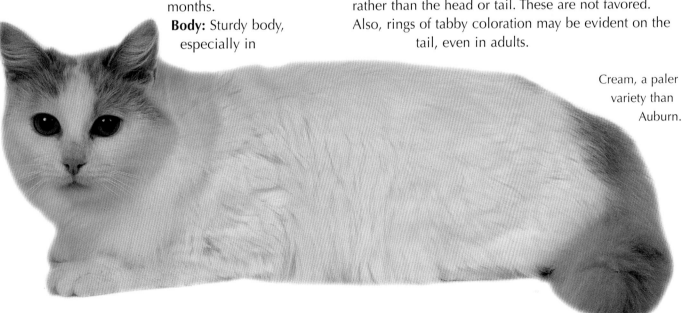

Cream, a paler variety than Auburn.

CAT ORGANIZATIONS

The American Association of Cat Enthusiasts, Inc.
PO Box 213
Pine Brook, NJ 07058
Tel: (973) 335-6717
Fax: (973) 334-5834
http://www.aaceinc.org/

The American Cat Fanciers Association (ACFA)
P.O. Box 1949
Nixa, MO 65714-1949
Tel: (417) 725-1530
Fax: (417) 725-1533
Email: acfa@aol.com
http://www.acfacats.com/

Canadian Cat Association
289 Rutherford Road,
S #18 Brampton, ON L6W 3R9
email: office@cca-afc.com
Tel: (905) 459-1481
Fax: (905) 459-4023
http://www.cca-afc.com./

The Cat Fanciers Association, Inc.
P.O. Box 1005,
Manasquan, NJ 08736-0805
Tel: (732) 528-9797
Fax: (732) 528-7391
http://www.cfainc.org/

FiFE-UK
Felis Britannica
29 Gunters Lane
Bexhill On Sea
East Sussex TN39 4EB, UK
Tel: +44 (0) 1424 732427
e-mail:
secretary@felisbritannica.co.uk
http://www.felisbritannica.co.uk/

Governing Council of the Cat Fancy
5 King's Castle Business Park
The Drove
Bridgwater
Somerset TA6 4AG, UK
Tel: +44 (0)1278 427575
email: info@gccfcats.org
www.gccfcats.org

The International Cat Association (TICA)
The TICA Executive Office
P.O. Box 2684
Harlingen, TX 78551
Tel: (956) 428-8046
Fax: (956) 428-8047
http://www.tica.org/html/english/home/

World Cat Federation e.V.
Geisbergstr.2
D-45139 Essen
Germany
Tel.: +49 201/ 555724
Fax: +49 201/ 554090
email: wcf@wcf-online.de
http://www.wcf-online.de/

FURTHER READING

Alderton, D. *Smithsonian Handbooks: Cats*, Dorling Kindersley, 2000

Bradshaw, J. *The Behaviour of the Domestic Cat*, C.A.B. International, 1992

De Prisco, A. & Johnson, J., *The Mini-Atlas of Cats*, T.F.H., 1991

Morris, D. *Cat World: A Feline Encyclopedia*, Ebury Press, 1996

Pond, G. & Raleigh, I *A Standard Guide to Cat Breeds*, Papermac 1982

Rixon, A. *The Illustrated Encyclopedia of Cat Breeds*, Blandford, 1995

Taylor, D. *The Ultimate Cat Book*, Dorling Kindersley, 1989

Warmer, P. *Perfect Cats*, Sidgwick and Jackson, 1991

Verhoef-Verhallen, E., *Encyclopedia of Cats*, Rebo Publications, 1997

Index

Index